Portrait Of A Man

To Ernest + Toji

Thanks For your

Love And support.

Eph. 3:20

Ted Alye

Portrait Of A Man

Book Of Poems

Ted Alan Dyer
ILLUSTRATED BY FLORENCE DYER

iUniverse, Inc.
New York Lincoln Shanghai

Portrait Of A Man
Book Of Poems

iUniverse, Inc.

For information address:
iUniverse, Inc.
2021 Pine Lake Road, Suite 100
Lincoln, NE 68512
www.iuniverse.com

Editor: Florence Dyer

Manuscript and Project Ted and Florence Dyer
Cover and Text Design:
Flo's Productions, Inc.
Graphic Artist: Florence Dyer
Cover illustrations: Florence Dyer
Inside Illustrated Sketches
By Florence Dyer.
All other Graphics are from Sierra Print Artist

ISBN: 0-595-29266-6

Printed in the United States of America

DEDICATION

To God, who is the head of my life.
I realize that it is in him that I live
and move and have my very being; as
certain poets have said, for we are also
His offspring's. (Acts 17:28 KJV)

Poet's Biography

Ted Alan Dyer was born and raised in Flint, Michigan. He graduated from Flint Northwestern high school. In 1979 immediately after high school he volunteered for the United States Navy. He was stationed in Great Lakes, Illinois. While in the Navy, he received 10 months of extensive training in the electrical engineering program. He sustained an injury during his training and was honorably discharged.

Ted's father Alfred Dyer, Sr. a self-employed cab company owner passed away at fifty-three, from bone cancer. Ted was three years of age when his father died. Ted painfully speaks only of a fleeting memory of touching his dads carefully folded embalmed hands. Ted has never been able to fill the void of the loss of his father. His writings speak of an emptiness he has for not having his father there. He learned very early that, when my father and mother forsake me, then lord will take me up.

(Ps. 27:10 KJV)

The Poet's mother Evelyn Juanita Dyer had both of her children in her late 30's. She worked hard to raised Ted and his one older brother Alfred, Jr. alone, after she was widowed at forty-three. His mother was born and raised in Meridian, Mississippi. She attended Alcorn University where she received a Bachelors Degree in Business Administration. After graduation she moved to Washington, D.C. and she was hired into the Pentagon where she worked for fifteen years. After leaving the Pentagon she made her home in Flint, MI, where she remained until she lost her battle for life to uncontrolled Diabetes. At the time Ted was 25 years old. Ted was very close to his mom and became very reclusive, because of the loss. Ted is very shy by nature and discovered writing to be a close companion throughout most of his life.

Ted first acquired an inspiration to write in the mid 80's from reading the bible. Ted met and married his beautiful wife Florence Juanita Dyer, in 1995. She shares in his love for writing and is a local Graphic artist. Together they have two children Daniel and Patricia. Ted values the closeness of his family.

Ted attended Baker College in 1996 to continue his pursuit in electrical engineering technology. He had to abandon the engineering training program once again to assume his first duties as a husband and father. He's had to continue working full-time as a press operator for a local engineering plant until June, 2002.

Ted attributes the inspirations of his writings to his wife and two children. He has watched his wife endure many physical hardships. Through her struggle of losing both of her kidneys to ESRD (End Stage Renal Disease) he has also had to painfully watch her undergo numerous surgeries She has endured years of hemo-dialysis, a kidney Transplant and CAPD (Peritoneal Dialysis). After CAPD she's now back on the list to be re-transplanted. In spite of her numerous health problems she is currently pursuing her Master's Degree online, and running their graphics company.

Ted's admiration for his wife's courage sparks the passion that is Inspired through his writings. He is also a great admirer of the late great Poets like John Keats, Edger Alan Poe and Byron Shelly. Ted has written numerous poems and songs. For years Ted's wife tried to convince him to publish His writings. He's now taking a Leap of faith standing on the word, Now unto him that is able to Do exceeding abundantly above all that we ask or think, according to the power that worketh in us.

(Eph. 3:20 KJV)

Ted is now forty-three years old and recently retired from working for many years as a Press Operator and later being promoted to Quality Control. Because of a neurological Disease that affects his vision he was forced to take an early retirement. Since retiring he has been given a greater opportunity to work full-time with his wife as a co-owner of Flo's Productions, Inc.

He serves as Vice President of Flo's Productions, Inc. assuming total responsibility as a freelance creative writer, Poet and treasurer. He has more time with their business and family. He's also, able to travel and develop his love for writing. Ted has found one steady philosophy that has ruled his life. That is *When one door closes another one always opens.* He has endured a lot of pain in his life but has always had one shoulder to lean on. Him and his wife both have a strong faith in God. Together the both of them have worked consistently to develop their creative gifts. Ted greatly hopes to increase the inspiration of his writings.

Through Ted's writings He conveys to the world, that no matter what a person has to endure, they can make it. Although it seems like at the time your going through there is no way out, or that it is all over, He lets you know that there is still hope. He expresses a lot of these thoughts in the poems entitled:
What is a Door, The Depths of Courage, When the Morning comes, Grace From Above, When Night Time Falls, Mountains Are Forever and Times Gone Bye. He also displays his affections for the love of his wife in the Poems entitled Angel Face, Morning Flower, The Little Lady, Black Girl, Black Girl, The Aroma of Her Love, Beauty of a Woman, Legs of a Woman and A Poem Of Love To The One I Love. A lot of the poems that express the pain he has felt over the loss of his parents are He Made Me remember my soul, Unseen Tears, When the Skies are Grey, Years Gone Bye, What is a Heart? and Is Death Better than life?

Ted derives a lot of his poetry from nature. This is seen very clear in a lot of his poems entitled:
When Autumn Comes, Flowers, Summer Weather, When Sunlight Shines and On Top Of Night Clouds. He also shares a lot of his personal inner struggles, during an intense journey of self-discovery. He describes his experiences in the poems entitled:
Me Myself and I, Begin the Day, Think I know the way, and The Birth of a Spirit.

PREFACE TO Portrait Of A Man: Book Of Poems

I faced some real challenges in putting together "Portrait Of A Man." Portrait Of A Man was birthed into my spirit at one of the most difficult trying times in my life. My wife was in the process of Facing another difficult surgery. I had been retired for a year and had physical challenges that I was facing myself. In spite of the Uncertainty of our future, I shared my dream with my wife and we were on our way. This is why I appreciate her and I thank the Lord everyday for blessing me with my best friend. She never Questioned my ability and we trusted God to open the doors.

A lot of the Poems have been revised and edited for distributions. Some of the poems were written during times of real distress while Working 8-12 hour days in an engineering plant. Having plenty of time on hand to observe the work environment. It has taken many years to develop the confidence to show a lot of my writings. Even though Portrait Of A Man is filled with a lot of my previously written Poems. They have been edited for publication. All artwork in Portrait Of A Man is not meant to be offensive in anyway. The female images are merely and artistic expression Of the awesome gift that the lord has placed within my Wife. It was a very difficult challenge getting Portrait Of A Man off the ground. By this being my first book my Wife and I were in a lot of prayer. We asked the lord to lead us in the Right direction, to bring about His will in our lives. We were in contact with several publishers and were very impressed with iuniverse. Soon we were off the ground and running. I firmly believe that anything worth having, is going to come with some form of opposition. We have defeated every challenge and are very satisfied with the final Results. Portrait Of A Man has challenged me to never give up on my Dreams. Now I challenge you to not give up on yours either, no matter what it looks like, no matter what stands in your way. I promise you as you begin heading in the directions of your dreams there is going to be a smoke screen. But keep on walking forward even if it is only an inch a day. Soon you will see the smoke screen, of what held you began to dwindle away.

My Darling Teddy,
I am so proud of you for stepping out into your destiny. You have always stood back and supported my dreams.
I have not wanted for anything that you have not bent over backwards to provide. No one knows the great sacrifices you made for us to have all that we have. It is because of you I have become everything that I am today. In the times I felt like I could not make it, you were there beside me; pushing me every step of the way. I am so grateful that the lord placed you in my life. Daniel, Patricia and me are all the better for you being apart of our lives. Now it is time for you to maximize your potential to the fullest. Reach out my Love and grab hold of everything that the Lord has for you. I know that releasing your writings was one of the hardest things you have ever had to do. The lord has given you an extraordinary gift to share with the world. But always remember what your release from your hands comes back to you in greater measures. We have to allow the lord to work, by giving him something to work with. I am so proud of you for finally getting the confidence to release the gift, I discovered in you from the first time we met. Now the world gets to meet the man I fell in love with. Your writings have been a great inspiration to me and I am sure that they will be a blessing to the world. Sweetheart as I said before, and I will say it again, Now you stand and be Blessed, My Mighty Man of Valor.
Love Always,
Your wife Florence J. Dyer

Artwork of: Flo's Productions, Inc.

I want to first give Glory and Honor to God for
Blessing me with such an extraordinary gift.
Next, I would like to thank my beautiful hard working wife
for the countless hours that she spent putting together My Book of
Poems.
She has dedicated herself day and night typing and editing each
poem.

I am so glad that she believed in me at times I did not believe in
myself.
She has remained steadfast and unmovable always abounding.
Throughout numerous battles with her health,
She has seen the project through to completion.
I would also like to thank my son and daughter
Daniel and Patricia for their love and words of encouragement.
In addition to my older
brother Alfred and his wife Gail.
I would also like to thank my cousin-in-law Bobbie Whitfield
For her loving support and words of encouragement, but most
importantly
for believing in me.
Your advice and friendship was just the motivation
I needed to pursue my dreams.
A very special thanks to my church family, of *"Gate of Heaven
Ministries."*
Special Thanks to the staff of Carlisle Engineering Products for years
of hard work from which my poetry derived.
I thank God for my Mother and Father Alfred and Evelyn Dyer,
for giving me life, without the both of you I would not be here.
I never knew that my pain would be an inspiration to so many.
Most of All I give God the Glory for blessing me
With an awesome gift to share with the world.
*A Mans Gift will make room for him
And bring him before great men.*
(Proverbs 18:16 KJV)

I pray that my Book of Poems "Portrait Of A Man," will be a blessing to
all that come in contact with it.

Ted Alan Dyer, 1979 USN

Portrait Of A Man

I hereby certify that all 100 of the poems listed are my original artwork.
They are each an honest and true effort of My personal creativity.

Contents

[When Autumn Comes]

When Autumn comes,
The sun shines bright
Through the Autumn trees.
The wind blows through the branches,
To the falling leaves.
Autumn is a time;
Of getting ready for the cold,
So the season goes around;
Like a story foretold.
What is to be,
Has already been,
Knock at the door and maybe;
He'll let you in.
The roots of the trees are as long
As a night.
The leaves that fall;
Autumn is a beautiful sight.
They float to the ground
Without a sound;
On a cushion of air they spin
Around and around.
The Rays of the Sun,
On the leaves they shine,
To change their colors,
What a beautiful sight is this time.
Season to season all for a cause,
In between seasons
There is never a pause.
The beauty of Autumn,
Is it all in my mind?
No Autumn
Is beautiful all of the time.
The beauty of the trees
Touches my desire,
All I want to do
Is sail higher and higher.
The beauty of the earth
Comes from up above,

From the father of lights,
The father of Love

A Poem On The Wandering Soul

Is there a soul that wanders and roams?
Tell me! Tell me! Does it have a home?
When those who see it
Is it really there?
Does it know what it sees?
Or is there any that care?
The way that it goes, no one knows.
It wonders on
Neither far nor near,
The soul is alive, the body is not,
Those that are around,
Look upon with a frown.
The faces are strange,
The places are not,
That, Which I would
That would I not.
Maybe that's how I ended up there?
Neither near nor far,
Please tell me where?
My body is thin just like the air.
Tell me! Tell me! How, when or where!
I am neither here
Nor there! Tell me!
Why, when, and where?
The days are long,
The nights are forever,
Tell me! Tell me!
Why must I still
Try to be clever?
Is it because of my being?
Or what I am seeing?
I'm neither here
Nor there! Tell me!
Tell me! Where, where, where?
The soul is deep,

Ted Alan Dyer

Deep as a well, For God's sake
Don't end up in Hell!
It is a place
You don't want to go,
It's a place
You don't want to know,
Some kind of way
I found my way back.
Thieves and robbers are everywhere,
They get on my nerves
And in my hair,
Do what you must, if you dare.
Time is short business
Is past due,
Don't wait too long
Or it all falls on you,
This is your day,
This is your way
Choose, Choose,
That you may
Not loose.

Angel Face

The one I love is my wife;
She was given to me as a gift of life.
From God himself,
And his ever unchanging grace,
That's why she's my Angel Face.
A Gift of Love
Sent from the father above.
For I know it is right,
For where have you been all of my life?
All my life, I've been running this race,
Looking high and low for my Angel Face.
Your smile is warm it lights up my face
And gives me Grace,
You're one in a million
You're my Angel Face.

Angel Face was recently selected for as a semi-finalist in the International Open Poetry Contest for $10,000. Also **Angel Face in addition to A Poem Of Love To The One I Love** will be published in the Eternal Portraits Fall Edition. Angel Face is currently featured on the following websites:

www.poetry.com

http://PostPoems.com/members/anface

www.Famouspoems.com

www.creativewriterscorner.com

Whoso findeth a wife findeth a good thing, and obtaineth favour from the lord (Proverbs 18:22 KJV)

Ted's Artist Profile

Poetry to me is a gift that inspires hope
To the lives of many people.
I first discovered my desire to write by reading the bible.
However my greatest
influence to writing poetry,
Has come through my
Wife and children.
Angel Face is a Poem that was inspired
Through the courage,
Strength and love,
I have seen my wife.
In spite of her physical health and adversities She continues to
Display a very strong will to survive.
I am always inspired through her
Never-ending love,
Support, warmth and gentleness, I see
Looking into her eyes, when in need of a miracle.

Is Death Better Than Life?

Is Death Better Than Life?
After Death is there any strife?
Where are you going?

Ted Alan Dyer

Up or down?
Do you really know?
Does this cause you
to where a frown?
Does life push you around?
Laughing as if you're a clown?
Are the days
as long as the nights?
For you, is life just one big fight?
Is Death Better Than Life?
Does the years go by
Quick and unseen?
Leaving you to wonder is the world really that mean?
Who's to know what was before? And what is to come?
No one in this world, that's under the Sun.
Do the days go by quicker then seconds?
Who is that?
Death, I believe beckons.
Death is something that comes from within itself.
Its comes
As if a life left on a shelf.
Is there any pain in this thing
That is so greatly feared?
Death is imminent,
Surely, there's no need for tears.
It must be done,
It's something
that must needs be,
Not only to thee,
But also to me.
It's often something taken for granted,
One thing for sure,
We must all leave this planet.
All I see is troubles and woes,
Tell me, tell me, why? Who knows?
Death is "Death Better Than Life?
Why is something so easy to obtain?
So hard to receive, maybe, maybe,
It's because of how you perceive.
Believing and perceiving

Are they both the same?
In whose heart?
And the rules belong to us,
Tell me, tell me,
Why is there a rush?
Life is but a moment,
Stop and enjoy it.
Is life, better than Death?
Who will you see when
You take your last breath?
I never expected
In my wildest dreams,
That this world
Was full of schemes.
Is Death, Better Than Life?

The Little Lady

Little Lady,
The little Lady
Made me her boy toy!
The little Lady
Is my pride and Joy—
The little Lady
Is there for me only
With the Little Lady
I'll never be lonely.
Little Lady,
The Little Lady
Is so strong and funny—
Her love,
The Little Lady
Is better than honey.
The Little Lady
Can Be Hard and Cruel;
The Little Lady,
Plays by her own Golden rules!
The Little Lady
Takes the straight and narrow.
With the little Lady

There's no maybe;
The Little Lady
For sure is my
Big, Big, Baby!
She's my Little Lady—
Brings no sorrow;
Me and My little Lady
Will always see
A Brighter tomorrow.
Me and My Little Lady;
being together is a must!
My sweet,
Sweet Little Lady—
Is fine; much finer than
The finest Gold Dust.
The Little Lady
And I were meant to Be!
The Little Lady
That was given as a Gift:
Was meant Just for Me.
T.A.D. 3-31-03

Mountains Are Forever

Mountains are forever,
Higher than the sky,
At the top—
Of every mountain;
Is an all Seeing Eye.
Mountains are Forever,
In this life you will truly see,
Till the great bye and bye
Reaching the other side,
Then will you become free.
Mountains are forever
The clouds make them their home,
Close to the stars also they roam.
Climbing up mountains
Is what life is all about,

Portrait Of A Man

Without these experiences
Life would be a never-ending doubt.
Day after day, night after night,
Week after week,
Tell me! Tell me!—whom do you seek?
The lightings are great,
The flashes are bright,
It can most surely shine
A path through the night.
Although the earth is very old,
And the tops of some mountains are very cold,
Covered with plenty of snow and Ice,
So the way of the world
Is not always nice.
Down in the midst
Are valleys and streams,
These are some places
Where people make dreams.
Covered with many
Trees, plants and flowers,
Climbing to the top
Takes many of hours.
Inside of the mountains
Are irons of old,
If you are fortunate you may find Gold,
Riches are there for those,
Whom they can find,
For those are the ones
That are one of a kind.
Diamonds and jewels
Also may be there,
Only the father knows
Exactly where;
All is the father's
They that know him
This is their belief,
Being his son,
Thank God what a relief.

Mountains are forever
Strong as steel,
Standing forever doing his will!

On Top of Night Clouds

The clouds of the night;
Seem to have a mind
Of their own!
Plotting their course
Through the skies:
They forever roam!
Clouds of the Night;
Floating in the air,
Have you ever wondered;
What holds them there?
On top of the clouds of the night,
The moonlight rays;
Shines its brilliant light.
Night clouds have a life of their own,
Always seeking traveling,
The forever skies are their home!
The night cloud makes you feel full of life
And I also envy,
Just like them;
I want to be floating;
Forever round the earth.
Night clouds form themselves;
Throughout the midst of time,
Sometimes they show and predict signs.
Clouds of the night;
Makes me want to live forever!
With the moonlight shinning on the top;
Reminding me of a land;
That's called never, never.
On top of night clouds;
My mind drifts away!
To a place called bliss,
Letting me know this world I will never miss.

On the top of night clouds;
My heart, my mind, and my soul they only see everlasting dreams,
That are all so possible,
They also have Golden seams,
Lined with silver,
And all and every precious gem and stone, never allowing me to forget
that one day I'll reach my heavenly home.
Roaming and passing through the bright and colorful stars of the
misty nights of our lives,
So beautiful and lovely
God must have meant them for our lives.
TAD 5-22-03

What is a Heart?

Inside of a Heart
There are feelings unknown,
Morals and values,
That must be sown.
The Heart was sent from God up above,
To those of the Earth,
The Heart that was sent,
His name was Love,
Love is powerful it sustains us all,
Yet most definitely without Love
We would fall.
The Heart and this emotion is all the same,
The Heart has a soul, which can be felt,
All of its virtues will never be known,
It also has a mind now that's one of a kind,
Joy and pain can dwell inside,
Some of the things that it needs to survive,
Your knowledge is great,
None can compare, grant me more,
Please don't ignore,
Humble and low is all I know,
Broken and torn I feel within,
Yet and still I'm not without sin.
The enemies' ways are diabolical and shrewd,
I need your strength in an intiment way.

When I look back, all I see is darkness
What is my life for? I know it came from you.
Life is short what must I do?
To see ahead I cannot comprehend,
Where does it end?
Why? where? And when?
Your ways are too great
For my mortal mind,
Trying to find out
Is just as if I was blind.
The Heart has a story that must be told
It's just like a riddle
Bought and sold.
The Heart is a book,
And also a door
Open it up is all for the more.
Look inside if you dare,
Quench the fire
And feel it smolder,
Trust in the father
And lean on his shoulder,
His strength is untold,
Everlasting, forever,
Strong and more than Bold,
The Heart has a spirit,
Which is strong,
Trust and believe
That it also has a song.

A Poem Of Love, To the One I Love

To the One I love the most;
In Heaven,
I know you'll be the host.
I love you more and more;
Each day.
You inspire me;
In each and every way.
With you problems seem so few.

I'm so Glad,
God blessed me with you.
You brighten up my Life,
In so many ways.
With You;
I want to spend all of my days.
When I wake up with you,
I'm always full of Joy.
Your Love makes me—
Feel like a Little boy.
I love you so much,
Words cannot say.
The way I love you;
We could never count the ways.
The depths of your love;
Have no measure.
It's just like searching;
For hidden Treasure!
I'm sure I'll Love You—
All of my Life;

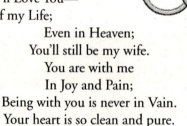

Even in Heaven;
You'll still be my wife.
You are with me
In Joy and Pain;
Being with you is never in Vain.
Your heart is so clean and pure.
Being with you
As a family,
Forever certainty—I'm sure!
(My Love is Forever)

Birth Of A Spirit

Is that just a spirit that follows the wind?
Which way does it blow?
Oh heavens sake;
Only the father knows,
In the earth is where it was put,
Strength and power
Is what it gives,

It comes from the father
To make you change,
With his spirit
All things are for sure,
Trust and believe,
That's all it takes,
His spirit can forgive
The shame of sin,
Cleanse me within,
Touch my soul,
Lead the way,
Show me what you feel,
is it real? Is it real?
It's Love from up above.
When sorrow filled my life,
and I became discouraged,
yet and still I was told to seek his face
for his ever unchanging Grace,
it kept my life in spite of me,
Death was my way—
that came upon me,
He opened his ears
and also saw my tears,
yet and still he made a way;
Protected me each and every day,
Even in the night
and in the day.
Day to day he made a way,
Close to him
Is a place I must stay,
To follow him
Is a wonderful task,
All things are new,
Old things are past,
Great is my life
All because of him,
His mercy is great,
With it I can stand,
None is able to pluck me
From his hand.

The times are late,
Yet he never changes,
He is forever;
Even though I've gotten older
He holds me together
And lends me his shoulder.
Fly away, Fly away,
Like an eagle I'll do someday,
far, far, far away
higher than the most distant star.
Trillion and trillion of miles away
to a bright and sunny day.
All my family and friends will be there;
Never a good bye will come to me,
What a glorious time that will be.
The father is there sitting on his throne, waiting to say son come
Home.
On the inside is a dream
That can be true just believe,
It's very important,
Please don't waste
Make no haste;
It's very important,
Please don't waste.
Great, Great,
That's what you are;
That's what I want;
No matter how far.

He Made Me Remember My Soul

He made me remember my soul, for he made me remember my soul. His love is as pure as fine gold, his riches are forever untold, to him will I commit my soul, for his love is as pure as fine gold. Although his wisdom through the ages are untold besides him there is no other, he sticks to me closer than any brother. His peace is calm and still I hope and pray to always stay in his will. For I know my faith in him will surely unfold. Even though his grace and mercy are of old, besides him there is no other, he sticks to me closer than any brother. His peace is calm and still I hope and pray to always stay in his will. For I know my life is in his care, with me I know he'll be with me everywhere, not to trust in him that not I dare. In him do I stand, for I know without a doubt he keeps me in his hands. For now I know I am in his master plan, so in his way I know I can. When death was certain I was filled with fear, his shoulder was there it was very near, always his spirit is there, no matter when no matter where. It is great it is fair, there is none that can compare, in him there is no time, so I know his heart must be mine, although his word is filling as kine, a home in heaven must be mine. When my enemies and my foes came against me, a sword on high will he give to defend me. His vengeance will comfort and protect me. His care makes me feel safe, for I know he is in every place. For I know also I will behold to see his face, for his ever-unchanging grace. Even though he knows I falter, he will ever keep me before his altar He is my courage in the face of danger, in him do I fear, and respect his anger. He is warmth when it is cold. With him I am always bold His knowledge is past understanding, His will is so demanding, but I know he knows what is best because of him I can rest. His word is true and fair, that is why, I know his righteousness is everywhere Even though everyone must trust and stand for those are the ones that will behold his hand the masters thoughts are strong and bold, for his strength is forever untold.

Although his spirit has no color, yet and still he sticks closer than any brother. His way has depths, yet I know I walk in all of his steps. His ways are always upon me, also, I know his judgments will ever go before me; his ways are all around me. Even though the way of his ways will cover me;

When different spirits come upon me. He never sleeps and he never slumbers. In his ways there is never a number. For I know his blessings are forever true and righteous. His angels are always near that is why there is never a need to fear on his shoulder  do I lean in a world that is wicked and mean. In him do I trust, that I must for without him I am just as the dust. The wind is strong it blows like a song, to and fro is the way it goes, it reminds me of my wonder-ing soul. He made me remember my soul; He made me remember my soul, for without him I am lost as a story untold. His spirit is Bold, it is for those who has been foretold the strength that he has will never past, it will last forever and ever, in that way there is never a never in that way there is rest, that is something you will possess. That way there is a will, it is not for enemies whose way is to kill. His way is quick, and it is sharp it touches the heart; it keeps you out of the dark. It is a light, trust and follow with all your might be strong because on this journey it's a hell of a fight. The race is long the race is hard just stand up and follow the trueness of His Heart.

The Depths of Courage

The Depths of courage;
reaches deep within
something that must be done;
no matter when,
the outcome is great,
no matter which way you take
Death is in the front,
and death is in the rear;
listen to that still small voice;
that speaks in your ear.
How did that occur?
Was it because of a deter?
Courage
is something that is deep
and long, also strong,
just like a smooth song.
Courage
is something that can't be seen;
with the naked eye,
without it you would most surly die.
It is something that is a very great need,
it must be there for each and every deed,
So you must take heed,
Courage is like blood,
it is a need.
Without courage your heart would bleed.
Death is for sure without this emotion,
You will surely die;
in the moment of a notion.
It is something that is possessive,
With courage you will be aggressive.
The way that it goes is strong and Bold,

it's essential in order to grow old.
Courage
is deeper than the lowest valley,
yet and still higher than the most distance star,
The way of its feeling will take you very far.
Its limits has no boundaries,
It reaches to the top and beyond the tallest of trees.
Without Courage
You will most surely fall—
to your knees.
Without courage
You will hide and run;
Without a reason,
This you will do in any season.
After you hide;
There will be no pride.
Pride is something
That is seen and felt,
Pride is always under your belt.
For without courage
there is no pride.
Courage
Is something that must be made,
It is sharp and strong as a sword's Blade.
It is hard and divine,
Divine as a will also strong as steal.
Without courage you can't be brave,
no valor is like darkness in a cave.
With Courage
There is no dark,
fearlessness is also found—
in the heart
with this life is right,
there's always light;
You'll feel ten feet tall,
Bold and Brave,
Life is a Ball.
Fearlessness is a must;
That must you have
In order to trust.

Valor is something
That must be earned,
As you get older;
This substance will be learned.

Grace from Above

Why does He Care?
He Cares—
Why does He Care?
Why does He Care?
The Days are very evil,
They've always been that way,
I've never opened my eyes to see,
The Greatness
That He has for me!
It's up to me to believe;
What he promised Me.
His love is too—
Great to Believe,
It is high, too high, to conceive.
His Grace has set me Free;
From the power of Captivity.
My Life was bound in Chains,
With a soul that couldn't rest,
With a soul that wouldn't rest.
Yet and still I gave my Best;
Yet and still I gave my Best,
My doubt and fears wouldn't let me rest,
All I tried was to give my Best;'
God's ways are eternal rest,
In His Grace
There is always rest.
The evil one my spirit he vexed,
Why did this happen?
I'll never know, His heart and his word is an open door; my mind is
open to His way,
Lead me guide me everyday;
His Supernatural world is there unseen,
The way of this world is full of schemes.

The Sun will rise at His command; the stars were created with His
hand,
The earth has pillars on which it stands,
Being righteous is the way you must go,
This is something that the devil does know,
Too and fro
Is the way he will go;
Looking for those
Who does not know;
The King of Glory;
For in His ways I must go!
Satan would have hoped
That I would have stumbled
And fell,
And ended up in
His eternal Hell!.
But God was there
To bind the Thief;
Jesus is the Christ——
What a relief!

When the Skies are Grey

When the skies are Grey
is there hope of a brighter way?
Does the sun only shine
On top of the clouds?
Looking for a way to break
All the way through;
To show the brightness of its rays,
that makes everything new.
The Sun and Clouds both were created by the same,
By His greatness
And within His name.
When the skies are Grey,
do you want to run and hide?
To a Place,
Where no one can surely see inside.
When the skies are Grey,

do your spirit begin to moan?
Looking for a better world;
To call your home.
When the skies are Grey,
What kind of love;
Takes away your pain?
When the skies are Grey,
There is a place
Where the sun shines
And there is never any rain.
The Father is the light
That shines,
Abundantly bright
Where there is never a night,
Never a night.
When the skies were Grey,
His son was killed,
Living His life doing his will.
The Greatest of us all;
None else was greater
Big or small.
Jesus Christ is his name,
He never changes; He's always the same.

Memories of a Friend

Memories of a friend of times gone bye,
They make me feel so good
I know that I can fly.
Memories of a song
and the memories of a dance,
the music sounds so good
it puts me in a trance.
The memories came back,
that I had forgotten all about;
they made my spirit soar
in the midst of a drought.
Memories come from within,
some come from above,
Memories can be sweet and soft,

They can float like a dove.
Memories for a friend
They can come at any time,
And in any kind of weather.
These are the memories
That are lighter than a feather.
Memories can make you smile;
They can also give you strength
To endure this life
To its fullest extent.
Memories can't be seen,
Only can they be felt.
Some memories of a friend
Become like fire
That may cause you to melt.
Friends and memories
Are both one in the same,
Depending upon the spirit
And in whose name.
Memories are forever
Some may say,
Maybe because they come
And go day by day.

Years Gone Bye

Time goes bye also very fast,
Yet and still in this life;
Very few things
Are here to last,
All is vain, all must past.
In this life—
We are destined by time,
Our fate is ours;
It's one of a kind.
My path is old;
It's already been foretold,
not only mine,
But yet and still;

Portrait Of A Man

Although has thine.
The ways of our end!
is only one of two ways,
all in all;
They're just numbered days.
Year's gone bye,
Can sometimes be sad,
The year's gone bye
Also can make you glad.
Knowing the Future is in God
And his care,
No matter why, when or where.
He knows my hurts,
and he knows my pain,
Although the years are gone bye he also knows my name.
My Heart skips a beat
For the years gone bye,
All must end
And that seems very right,
Because of the year's gone bye every hurt and every pain must eventu-
ally die.
Because of the years gone bye
There will be a greater day.
All is seen by God
and his all seeing eyes, he's strong, not like the father of lies.
T.A.D.2-5-03

Me, myself and I....

I am myself;
is there more than me?—If so
Then on my way I will Go.
It is I, Is it Me?
Who am I?
Is it thee?
It is I!
It is thee!
Who am I?
Or is it We?
We both are the same.

So is the Name;
Is this me? Tell me!
This is not a Game!
We are One; at the same time?
Or are we twine?
My spirit is mine?
Why must it be
More than one of a Kind?
I am Me!
Or is it He?
Something I must know!
Or is it We?
This is something,
I've known all the time.
It was unleashed,
But not for the first time.
Me and My self are One.
Life is real; It's not a Joke!
It was something spoken.
I am something more than I see.
Believe Me,
Believe Me, it is thee;
My body is here. It is always near.—
Where am I? Where am I?
Am I right here?
I am strong! I am Bold;
even when the day is cold!
One day my breath will surely seep,
the way of the spirit is very deep.
I am me, I am thee,
Who is it, is it we?
We both are, the same tell me, tell me.
Under whose name;
I am here;
I am there, tell me, tell me!
I want to know.
Where did He come from? Does
He exist, did he materialize—(This I insist)
There are some things;
I do not know;

Portrait Of A Man

I am more than one
This is for sure.
This thing has happened!
I don't know why;
Is it because of what I thought?
Was not a lie?
This is Me! This is we!
It is I; It is thee.
When I go, when I come;
To where to from.—
Physical matter is here;
Maybe far, or maybe near
The mind is here;
The mind is there,
The mind is everywhere
Maybe far or maybe near. The mind is here, the mind is there; the
mind is everywhere;
Maybe near, maybe far;
Even unto the
Most distant star.——
What must I do what must I do?
Tell me, tell Me; it is you?
I am alive, Am I dead?
Tell Me, Tell Me
Is this all in my head!
Am I young? Or am I old?
This is a story that must be told——
My flesh is old, my soul is new.
So is my spirit and so are You.
My future is old;
My past is new!
Looking towards the future
Is something I must do.
The way that I look
Is just for me;
I love myself and so do we.
Me and myself, we are divine; we are most definitely
One of a kind!
My blood is warm;
My skin is soft.

What about my spirit?
Does it go aloft?—
My thoughts are mine! Or are they twine? Who are thee or is it we. I
talk to myself.
Just like thee! is it Me? Or is it He? Thee is he and so are we. I left my
body and
Went for a walk.
He even had the nerves to talk.
The things He said;
I did not like at all
He tried to set me up; for a Fall.
I am me; He is He:
it is We, or is it thee.
I am we, we are thine,
Life gets better;
Aged like the finest of wine.
My life is mine;
Not for thee!
It is judged only of He.
He sees my Heart;
He knows my mind! The things
That I do are one
Of a kind.
The inside is felt
The outside is seen
Is it because the world is mean?
I am myself;
I am one man!!
There is no excuse
For me to stand!
My life is not an obsession;
But in this world you must show
Some aggression!

Me, Myself and I is an outer body experience about self-discovery of
the Holy Spirit dwelling on the inside of me. I was discovering the
reason for existence. Knowing that there is an invisible force that gov-
erns our natural existence. Trying to figure out how human existence
came about and where we go once we leave this Earthly existence.

What Is A Thief?

Is there a thief
That cannot be seen?
He is the one
who is there to glimmer and glean;
His way is Cold,
Also Bold and very old!
Through his way wisdom will surely unfold.
No one knows his name;
His way is a Game;
He only looks for Fame;
Which Always leads to Shame!
His ways are there;
They are everywhere—
It is You whom he seeks;
For he looks within
For a part of you.
That may be weak.
The way of his ways
Are at large
By those who knows the most about the Host.
For he is death,
his sword your see, is in a sheath.
On you it he will use
As a tool to abuse.
In His way you will smoother,
He claims to be your brother.
That way is hard,
It's like pulling at random—
—A playing card.
He is a empty heart
Without a part.
Its way is unknown;
Without a home;
For always he must roam.
All alone.
The strength that he has
is but for a season,
Doing things speedily,

For that is His reason.
It is of none effect,
Unable to detect.
The Thief, His time is forever,
In that there is no pause,
So those ways
Are without a cause.
Yet and still if you get lost,
Always go north
And follow the moss.
For it leads to the light,
The way, which is always right,
Follow with all your might.
Deceitful and deadly
The way of the heady.
With him more than poor
Will be to score.
Cold as ice,
Deceiving by being nice.
To steal is that will,
Also to kill and made ill.
That way is quite contrary,
Like a night walk
In the cemetery,
Quite as can be,
Without a sound
Nothing you'll hear
Not even see.
Without him there is no time,
For he is the way of the world.
Old and Wise, him you
Will despise.
For he is only there, to demise.
The God of this world
Is my surprise;
Round and round
What's the more?
The world is a revolving Door. 5-24-03

What Is A Door?

What is a Door?
Where does it lead?
Does it help those—
Who are in need?
Is there a Door—
That can't be seen?
When it is open—
Is that side of life mean!
Will you get older?
Or will there be a need—
For a shoulder?
When the Door is closed;
What will you see?
How was it opened?
Was it because of thee?
Are there any regrets?
Nevertheless,
Did it also bring frets?
The Door can be cold,
And also can make you bold!
Those that are within,
Are they really what you see?
Or are you aggressive,
in order to be possessive?
When the Door is closed,
What do you feel?
Are there others still trying to steal?
The door is of the Chief,
it keeps you away from the thief.
Its also a will,
does it lead to the steal?
Round and round some Doors may go,
it never stops,
did you know?
Health and wealth
May be inside,
The choice is yours to decide.
Behind the Door

Ted Alan Dyer

There is knowledge and power,
Something you must seek,
Hour after hour.
When you find it,
You'll stand
As if you were a tower.
It comes as a rain,
There's no need to complain.
Hand in Hand
You must do what you can;
To remain in the land.
Behind the Door
There is light,
Open and seek it—
With all your might.
The land of the light,
You'll get there.
With a flight;
To a place where there's
Never a night.
It is of the more,
it is of
The door, north, east, south
And west, there
Is also a door in my heart.
There is a door;
That is full of Grace,
It will never be closed-in your face.
The Master is within,
The Master is without,
With the master;
You'll never be without.
The days are forever,
The nights are never,
There is never cold,
You will never get old.
There's no need to be spoken,
For the door is always open,
on the inside is what you own,
Because of him;

Who sits on the Throne.
T.A.D. 5-1-03 5:00 p.m.

Times Gone Bye

Times gone bye
seem to make you wonder why?
Days seem long and so does the nights.
Is life just one long fight?
Life has rules,
so does everything else;
don't lay your life on a shelf.
Riches and wealth will come
And sometimes go,
How important are these things,
Who is there to know?
What is the purpose, what is the reason? These things can come and
these things can go, for any reason also in any season. Time is of the
essence I heard it once said, for this reason
Don't spend your life sleeping,
Or you may find your self
On your death bed;
In times gone bye I wonder why,
I find myself looking up towards the sky,
Looking for a place I never before seen,
Trying to escape a world
that is wicked and mean.
My life goes bye as a cloud in the air, where is it going? who in this
world cares. In times gone bye chances
come and chances go,
will they come again
Who is there to know?

The Aroma Of Her Love

The Aroma of her love is pure as milk,
sweet as a dove,
Smooth as silk,
For sure it came down from above.

The Aroma of her love is there for the taken, my heart,
Her love starts it to quacking, and my spirit shaken.
The fragrance of her love it melts my soul,
my heart and my soul is refined as Gold.
The Aroma of Her Love
takes me to
Heaven where I forever want to be,
Her Love fragrance blinds my mind of all else;
Only hers do I see.
The Aroma of her love is free as the wind,
Also to her love, my heart will forever bow,
And my spirit will always bend.
Her Love and Her fragrance is thin as the air,
it ascends higher than the clouds without a care.
The Aroma of her love,
Comes from deep within Her heart,
Especially from each and every inner part.
The Aroma of her love is pure and clean,
Through her fineness,
Though the pureness of her fragrance is often seen.
Her ways are great, greater than grand,
Her ways are so sweet she feeds me from her
hands,
The Aroma of her love is fresh,
Fresher than fresh,
All the while I'm together with her,
Her body I forever want to caress.
Her love is so valued,
Worth more than ten lifetimes,
Thank God our body, spirit and
Soul will eternally entwine.
The fragrance of her love keeps me alive,
Makes me live,
For the Aroma of her Love, my life I would give………….

Begin the Day, I think I know the Way

Begin the day,
I think I know the way.

For my steps are ordered by God,
Each and every day.
All because of the prayers I pray.
So I know my prayers are heard,
Because He guides me
With his word.
Throughout the Land
Of the living,
Most surely
His grace is for the abundance
Of the giving.
I think I know the way,
His word He gently whispers
In my ear,
He walks beside me.
Which comforts me all so dear.
So I begin the day I think I know the way,
the way that he leads,
Within my heart is so sweetly seen,
Through troubles and dangers unseen,
in a world that can be wicked
And mean. I begin the day,
So I think I know the way,
His spirit is a lamp unto my feet,
Although it is his face that I seek.
Because of his love I am very meek.
Yet although,
The warmth of his love keeps me humble,
In the light of the father;
I will never stumble. Begin the Day,
I think I know the way.
T.A.D.3-19-03

Inside the Forest

Inside the Forest,
Is there a place
Where you can call home?
There deep inside there is peace,
Joy and happiness unknown.

Ted Alan Dyer

Inside of the forest when it rains your heart
Is sure to get wet,
The forest it self is always warm so warm
You're sure to sweat.
Deep, Deep,
in the midst of the Forest
Is life that's just waiting
To come forth, Inside of this
Forest is love the deeper you go
Even east, west, south and north.
The Forest is life, and has a fragrance all of its own, the fragrance
is heavenly sent giving you all the comforts of home.
The Forest has a food that's one of a kind
The food once it is eaten,
Cast a spell forever
You'll seek till
Your tongue
Will only want to find.
The taste is sweeter
Than honey, purer than milk,
It taste as the way of love,
Smooth as silk. Inside of the Forest is a burning fire piercing your
heart,
Spirit and soul,
Feeding your desire.
Inside of my forest
Is soft gentle goodness
That gives life to all inside of the forest you'll forever fall, the trees are
thick and
Very tall, everyone under them seems very small.
The nectar of the plants
And trees
Are that of a virgin girl,
Her fragrance is in the air making it swirl.
Ted Alan Dyer 5-10-03

When Nighttime Falls

When nighttime falls
Is there a place to call home?
Or throughout the earth will you forever roam.
Throughout the darkness
Is it so thick?
It has become a part of thee?
When nighttime falls
Does your soul seems lost
And without any hope,
Causing you pain
Unbearable and inability
With your fears
You're unable to cope.
When the nighttime falls,
Does the gloom of tomorrow
That you think will come
Cause you nothing but despair,
Leaving you to wonder
Will anyone ever begin to care?
When the nighttime falls
Does the world seem colder?
Sometimes than it actually is.
Once the darkness has come
Does God show you that all belongs To him?
And that all is his.
When the nighttime falls
Is there a spark that glimmers?
Letting you know
That the darkness
Is not lasting forever, when the night time falls
Does the moonlight cast a spell?
Giving you courage and the strength
To endure any and
All kinds of weather.
Is there a spirit in the night?
Giving you expectations to a brighter and a more abundant day,
touching and warming your heart also whispering
All so gently in your ear giving

You guidance and leading you in the right way.
Ted Alan Dyer 5-9-03

Summer Weather

Summer Weather is the nicest time of all,
its very pleasant much nicer than fall.
The Summer Weather mostly is for reunions
With family and friends, and sharing summer games
Meeting new people and not forgetting their names,
The weather in the summer is sometimes misty, and mild,
It can feel so good
You'll feel like a child.
Summer Weather is chilled at night, sitting and telling stories around
a campfire,
And being warmed
By the firelight.
Summer Weather,
Changes a lot just as the seasons in which we live, the weather at this
time makes us all
Want to give.
Summer weather is breezy
And cool not ever
A hint of smog,
Rainy, misty weather sometimes brings a thick, thick fog.
Ted Alan Dyer 5-16-03

When Sunlight Shines

When the sunlight
Shines brightly
And the day is
Bright and sunny,
These are the times that can't be bought with
Any amount of money.
When the Sunlight Shines
And all is crisp and clear,
And the clouds are so close
You can touch them

They seem just that near,
The Sun is shinning,
The birds singing and all is well,
The events
Of the day have a spirit
That seems to cast a spell.
When the sunlight shines,
And dreams seems all so near and easy to be made,
When the sunlight shines
And the shadows
Seem to disappear,
The trees bend and
Weep without shedding a tear.
When the sunlight
Begins to show its ways,
The brightness of the lights shines for days and days.
When the Sunlight shines,
The whole world begins to smile,
Even the moon and all the stars,
They're happy as a newborn child. (T.D. 5-21-03)

The Beauty of a Woman

The Beauty of a woman
is very great.
Touch her heart
Before it's too late.
Her
Skin is as smooth as silk,
Her love is pure
And sweet like milk.
It is the Beauty of a
Woman, her legs are long and Beautiful,
They make my heart melt like wax,
It's just like Heaven
And that's a fact.
Something I wish I new;
in times gone by.
Something to cherish;
Need not ask why.

Her passion is strong
It shows in her eyes,
For God's sake my longing
Is to be between her thighs.
In between her thighs,
Her aroma is sweet,
Why?
Only God Knows!!
Yet and still
May I give her my
Heart,
That it may be we'll never part.
Her Beauty is far
Beyond all the words I can say,
Her smile
Is just like a bright
And sunny day.
Her lips are all so soft
And so are her breasts.
All I feel is compelled to do
Is to kiss her and forever caress.
Her feet are soft they even have
a soul, her toes are all numbered
Like cherries to be plucked
They look so good
Making me desire to kiss
This is my luck.

The Legs of a Woman

The legs of a Woman
Are soft and smooth.
The legs of a Woman
Will steal your heart,
Like a morning star
And a desire flickering;
to start.
Her legs and her beauty—
Were sent from above,

They are pure as her fragrance
Which is of love.
Her scent is strong and also sweet,
in between her legs is a Heavenly-treat.
Within her legs
There's strength unknown,
Their power
and their beauty
my soul they surely own.
My heart burns with an unquenchable fire, all
Because of the beauty of her desire.
Out of my eyes all that I can see,
are her thighs;
Ever the more sexy-as can be.
Breaking me down,
Down to my knees, so that
All I want to do is to beg her
And say, pleaseeee—
Deep down in between is a power divine,
That's where my heart,
Spirit and soul longs to be;

All the time.
Inside is a food forever more,
Push the right button
And she may open the door.
Nothing known on earth
is better to a man,
Giving me the compassion
To eat from her hand.

Her legs are all so very strong
And meant to be cherished,
Without them to gaze upon;
I would most surely perish.

[When the Morning Comes]

When the Morning Comes,
Will the day bring daylight?
Or will it bring rain?
When the Morning Comes,
Will your name be the same,
Or will it change?
When the morning comes,
Will you feel like rising to see………..
Another day?
Or will you go on about your business;
Never thinking to pray.
When the Morning Comes,
Will you touch my heart?
With a kind word and a smile?
Letting me know,
With me you'll go the extra mile.
When the Morning Comes
Will you kiss my cheek when I'm sad?
When all the world seems as if it's mad?
When the Morning Comes will you still be my friend even though
sometimes all we do is argue, fuss and fight;
Although the nights are very cold and we feel all alone leaving us to
wonder is this world really our home?
When the Morning Comes,
Will we still see eye to eye,
And look deep, deep, down on the inside, and under our breath won-
der why must there be death?
When this life is over will we still know each other,
Will I always be your son?
And you forever be my mother.
When the Morning Comes,
Will I still feel your love?

Portrait Of A Man

Coming down from above,
Descending upon my heart, spirit, and soul,
Like a story of old,
That has already been foretold;
From the beginning of time,
Our love together
Will always intertwine.
When the Morning Comes,
Will the stars still be hanging
In the sky?
As a gateway
To the Great Bye and Bye,
And the clouds
Looking like pillows floating in the air soft
And fluffy without a care.
When the Morning Comes,
And the night has past away,
And our spirits have become one,
And our rest has come and gone.——
Thank God, we have a Heavenly Home.
When the Morning Comes
And the sky is bright and clear,
I will always hold your memories dear.
When the Morning Comes
When the Morning Comes:
Is Dedicated in memory of my mother Evelyn Juanita Dyer
(1923-1985)

Tears

Does life bring you times;
That causes tears to flow from your eyes?
Leaving You feeling guilty, but giving you wisdom in order to make
you feel wise.
(Tears)
Do they show the pain on your face?
Because we live And run
to endure this race.
(Tears)

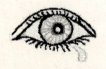

Are there days tears fall from your eyes more than the rain—
That fall from the skies;
Giving you a reason to believe;
They will not stop until you die.
(Tears)
Do they cover you with shame?—
Sometimes causing you;—to be confused!
And in doubt
Of which way to Go.
(Tears)
Is there any fear in your heart;
Because of tears—You have shed?
Leaving you tossing and turning all night!
And causing you to live with nightmares!—While lying in bed.
Were there times when you felt so sad?
That all you could do;
Is think about the things—
You wish you had?
[Tears]
Can often bring gifts and blessings;
But most of all
The shedding of tears;
Teaches us lessons.—
Tears!
T.A.D. 4-23-03

Wishing On A Star

Do you spend your life wishing on a star?
Always having a Dream and taking it with you everywhere you go no
matter how far.
Wishing On a star;
Do your Dreams seem to be a distance away that they may never
come true?
Leaving you wondering how to make them happen and what it is that
you must do?
Wishing On a star;

Are you looking towards the future no matter what believing that
your dreams will surely come to past, hoping and praying the sadness
and waiting will fade away all so fast!
Wishing on a star;
Have your wishing and your hoping taken you to the edge of heaven,
the Gates of Pearl and the streets that are made of Gold;
The wishes that you have do they remain in your heart waiting for
you to take a stand and live a life as a story that just has to be told!
Wishing on a Star;
Do your Dreams fade away when the morning light begins to shine?
Are they sometimes tossed to and fro by those that you thought that
you have left behind. If so never stop dreaming and wishing all things
can come true;
Just hold on with all of your might and all things are possible for you.
4-23-03
Ted Alan Dyer, 2003

Friends

Is there someone there
You can depend on?
When times get tough,
All the while the only thing;
You need is a smile
And the problems
Wouldn't seem so rough.
Friends;
Are they really what you need?
To let you see
What life has in store?
Tell me!
Are they really a friend, or are they just waiting for you to prosper and
let them in by opening up a door?

Friends;
Are they around to comfort you?
Or pretend and wait for you to turn your back;
If so do you feel you know enough—
Not to fall for that act!
Friends;
Have they been exposed
And allowed you to see who they really are?
Although, throughout the years you suddenly realize from them you
have been very far.
Inside of their heart is nothing but deceit and lies;
Pretending to Care.
But, all the time hiding the truth from your eyes.
Friends;
The Cruelness that they have is all that is seen and their compassion is
nothing but always full of lack;
Leaving you to wonder
Should you think before you turn your back.
Friends;
Are they what you need?
If not take heed!
And then ask yourself;
The Blood of Christ do they plead!
T.A.D. 4-22-03

Chains Of Our Lives

Are there chains on your life, holding you down?
Wrapping themselves around your soul keeping you from being;
Heaven bound?
Chains of our lives
They are often created
By the things we despise.
Chains they come to us promising wealth-yet and still they deceive
and take away our well being;
And finally our health.
The lack of wisdom can put us in despair and the chains that life may
bring, leaving us sad,
Lonely and a happy song

Were unable to sing.
Chains have always been there to enslave!
Creating nothing but desolation and making your home to seem like
a cave.
Chains in our lives are something that should not be;
Blinding our minds and our hearts preventing us from feeling free and
being able to see.
The chains of our lives may bring doubt and fear,
Causing our pains and
Making our tears.
Chains can be broken by the power
That we have within,
Breaking the shackles and
Allowing God to wash away our sins.
Chains, they can take away our freedom,
Put us in prison,
Kill our vision,
But thank God Almighty that the Savior is, Risen!

[Black Girl, Black Girl]

Black Girl, Black Girl!
Your eyes are like the most precious of pearls.

Black Girl, Black Girl!
Your skin is so fair;
It makes me want to touch you—Everywhere.

Black Girl, Black Girl!
Where was I—when you were born?
Maybe I wasn't even thought of,
I was still being formed!

Black Girl, Black Girl!
Your beauty is so great,
Your love, your love;
I want to take.
Give it to me freely, please!
For you I want to forever;
Be on my knees.

Black Girl, Black Girl!
Your breasts are so sweet,
Sweet as a pear;
So is your navel—
May I touch it with my tongue
If you dare?

Black Girl, Black Girl!
Inside of your heart
—Is a love unknown?
All I want to do is make your heart
—My home!

Black Girl, Black Girl!
Your love is rich and very lavish—

Black Girl, Black Girl!
You I want to ravish.

Black Girl, Black Girl!
The fragrance of your love;
Makes me want to fly away!
With you as my flower;
To a never ending bright and sunny day.

Black Girl, Black Girl!
God gave you life;
Thank God! Thank God!
About Me, You didn't think twice!

Black Girl, Black Girl!
Your skin is so dark;
And purer than pure.
Your life is that of a Queen
And that is for Sure.

Black Girl, Black Girl!
Your colors are many,
The love that you can give;

Is more then plenty.

Black Girl, Black Girl!
At Your feet I long to be!
Adoring your beauty;
Is all I can see.

Black Girl, Black Girl!
Your legs and your thighs;
Are worth more than pure Gold;
Up in between is a story untold.

Black Girl, Black Girl!
More than Heaven;
Is what you have inside;
Without your love;
I want to run and hide.

Black Girl, Black Girl!
Sweeter than honey,
Fresher than a flower;
With you I want to be;
Every hour!
T.A.D. Revised 5-22-03

Flowers

Flowers,
They grow and bloom;
Flowers,
They touch the heart;
Like a Bride and Groom!
Flowers,
Are light and sunshine
When the day seems
Filled with so much gloom.
Flowers,
They themselves;
Are full of fragrance;
And fresher than fair,

The aroma they release;
Belongs to the Air!
Flowers,
Beautiful and Bright
The life they illuminate
Lights up the night.
Flowers
They themselves
Seem to be a woman's best friend;
Springing from their hearts
And deeper from within.
Flowers,
I believe can be said
To have a will of their own;
Making their lives to dwell in our houses and our homes.
Roses I've heard
It to have been said are a girls best friend—
A means to a beginning;
But often an end!
Glimmering like Gold,
In the eyes of many.
Flowers,
The variety in which
They come certainly are many.
Plenty of sizes,
Plenty of shapes, the fragrances and aroma's you breath
They will surely awake.
Sold for fortunes given for love,
They can melt your heart
And cause your spirit to fly away;
Like a dove
Flowers they themselves
Bring nothing but smiles,
Lighting up your eyes.
Also they can make you say,—
Please!
The beauty that they can bring;
Can break you to your knees.
They bloom, blossom,
And sprout,

Throughout the season;
Even when there is a drought.
Flowers,
Have a soul just like you and I!
Flowers,
Follow us to Heaven;
Flowers;
Will never die.
5-22-03

Is Life A Dream

In this life that we live
Is it hard to believe—?
That it may be a dream?
Is what we feel and see, what it really seems?
Who's there to know?
When we awake,
Which is the right way to go?
Who's in control, of your path and the way of your soul?
Those that are around,
Are they really there?
Are they just a figment?
Or do they really care?
Is a dream just an emotion
Created in a notion?
To keep life
And the heart in motion?
What is a dream?
Thoughts in your sleep—
How are they formed?
Is it really that deep?
Through the oracles of time,
Divine in wisdom,
Straight from the heart,
Soul and mind.
More real than reality some dreams may seem.
Some may have fear and
Some may have schemes.
Inside of a dream

Do you ever feel alone?
Then stand by and observe while your inner self roam;
A will of its own.
Some dreams possess,
Looking into the Future
While you rest.
Is life just A Dream?

Have You Ever Been Right?

Have you ever Been Right?
When everything says
Your wrong!
Claiming that all you do is sing
The same old song?
Did they ever stop to think?
To stop and take a look
At themselves;
Also do their thoughts and their
Actions add to your wealth?
Are their ways
And their feelings all
Full of pride?
Waiting and trying to push
You aside.
Thinking that your thoughts
And your
Ways are not really true;
Making you so angry,
You don't know what to do.
Causing you to believe;
That your fate
Maybe filled with hate,
Sometimes you feel so ill
That You may abandon the divine will.

Holidays

Holidays
Are times when families should come together
Holidays
They are meant for everyone;
In all kinds of weather!
Holidays
They Honor special events
And special occasions,
Which affects our influence
And causes persuasions.
Holidays
Times and events by history they have grown;
Opening up doors we have never known.
Holidays
Ordinary days are from which they came;
Given added responsibility
Is how they earned their name,
More than many are these special days;
That we celebrate
Holidays
Always their own time
For they will truly never arrive late.

Rainy Day

When the days are rainy
And the skies are cloudy and Grey.
For one thing I know
—Within myself;
That the shinning of the Sun
Will always bring
A brighter day.
Rainy Days,
Must come to us all,
Throughout the spring,
Winter and fall.
Days that are Rainy
And bleak also filled with gloom,

Yet and still this is never any good reason to stay locked away hiding
from your doom.
Rainy Days, the doom that you thought would arrive, so it never
came, and the opposite was in your favor to keep you alive. Days of
old and Days of new, they come in many fashions;
So now I know they all are the same,
So now what must I do?
Rainy Days, most certainly they have a spirit and a soul all of their
own,
Rainy Days,
With their own personality and in certain seasons is where more
clearly they decide to stake their home.
On days that are
Rainy the clouds are shedding tears,
Filling the earth with what it needs to survive for years and years.
Rainy Days are yours,
And Rainy Days are mine,
Did you also know that
Rainy Days
Are also filled-with plenty of sunshine.
The Rays of the Sunshines through the gloom, tell me why, would
you want to stay hid away in your doom.
The doom that you perceived never came,
The father of Lights
Washed it away in His name.
TAD 5-3-03

Butterfly

Butterfly, Butter Fly
Floating in the air,
So when I see you it seems you
Never had a care.
Floating so freely on an invisible cushion of breath, you seem as if
you'll live forever because of your Beauty, and you're much prettier
than death.
Butterfly, Butterfly,
In Heaven
You must have been made,

You glide on wings of Gold, Silver and Diamonds, and the Great
Cedars of Lebanon you have made your home,
And your place of shade.
Butterfly, Butterfly,
Flying and floating;
For within the air has always been your home,
You were born in the treetops
So within the midst of them you must forever roam. You must have
inherited happiness,
If you weren't in the world,
Tell me please what would I do?
Your body is so soft,
Frail and tender,
You were created so beautiful,
I can't even tell your gender.
Butterfly, Butterfly,
For within you I know you have a spirit and a soul, the way you glide
through the air is far more valuable than the world, and all of its pre-
cious stones and its finest and purest Gold.
Butterfly, Butterfly;
Fly, Fly, Flyaway.
When you reach your everlasting Golden Home, Ill know we are just
alike for we both remembered to pray.

Eyes Of The Night

Are there eyes in the Night;
That seem to follow you no matter
Where you may go?
Eyes of the Night
Who do they belong to?
Where did they come from?
Who's To Know?
But yet and still they seem
To watch you from head to toe!
Night Eyes
Are always there
Sifting your soul!
Often cold
As the sleet, rain, ice and snow.

Eyes in the Night
Are in the midst of time;
Always they've been in existence
Who do they belong to?
Behold they're yours and Mine!
Eyes in the Night
They can pierce your soul;
Look into your spirit
And cause you;
To never grow old!
Eyes in the Night
Are like the laws;
That are unseen,
They're to judge your heart
And your life
They must redeem!
Eyes Of The Night
Often are looking
Into the unknown;
Belonging to forever
The darkness
Is their home!
Eyes Of The Night
Are always looking into eternity;
Forever is their home;
Throughout the Universe;
They will always roam.
TAD 4-23-03

Dragonfly

Dragonfly, Dragonfly
Your home is always beyond the skies;
You float on a cushion of air
Right before my very eyes.
Flying through the atmosphere;
You move so fast
A sound I cannot hear.
Dragonfly, Dragonfly,

Your wings are made of steal,
Your heart and your mind seems to have
Its very own will.
Although your eyes are just like lights;
Yet and still, you see all you were meant for was to protect your home
and fight. Dragonfly, Dragonfly,
Your life will never end, most surely your more than a conqueror for
each battle you will most surely win.
Dragonfly, Dragonfly,
You're a warrior
Of stories untold,
Your strength and your power show us all
That truly you are very bold.
You were created by the hands of man, For God gave us this knowl-
edge to live and
Dominate the land.
Dragonfly,
Your way is that
Of a burning fire,
So it is your desire;
That takes you
Higher and higher.
For most surely
The Universe is your home,
For we all know
That's where you will forever roam.
T.A.D 4-1-03

Mother Earth

Mother Earth, Mother Earth;
What is your value?
For who knows your true worth
Mother Earth, Mother Earth;
How were you hung on the pillars of
Nothingness?
Hanging in the middle
Of outer space
On neither air nor atmosphere

Your creator is greater
than grand;
For all was created by the master's hand.
God Himself his fingers created all of
The stars and gave them all names, they are just like children having
fun and playing games.
Mother Earth, Mother Earth
Grand, Great, and everlasting;
Strong and powerful your own shadow is what you are casting—
Spinning your way round and round;
Quiet as can be you never make a sound.
Mother Earth,
A heavenly body you are without a doubt, the fight that was fought
I'm sure was a real hard bout.
Surrounded by stars and planets;
Saturn, Venus and Mars.
Your Beauty is forever;
Mother Earth, Mother Earth,
Your ways are full of joy and;
That's all you bring, your goodness makes
Me want to live forever and do nothing but dance and sing.
T.A.D. 5-5-03

Temptation

Temptation, Temptation,
Comes to us all;
One thing for sure;
If you're not careful
Temptation
Will cause you to fall.
Temptation
Is great, endurance is stronger with the ability to endure your life for
sure will last much longer.
Temptation and endurance there one in the same;
Both are opposite of one another;
They both have a game.
Stick and stay; endure, endure and temptation will go away.
Temptation

Is as of a desire; a burning fire, waiting to be fueled by the Heart and it's Desires.
So it seems temptation is strong;
Rather it be right
Or wrong.
The world is filled with tempting pleasures, only true; endurance will bring you their treasures. The life of endurance brings no grief; its treasures and pleasures take us from our sins, it's a great relief. The wages of Temptation most surely will take your breath,
The end result;
Is nothing but death.
T.A.D. 5-3-03

Tomorrow

What is Tomorrow?
Can it be seen?
On Tomorrow, is it a day in which you want to go away?
Is it full of troubles and problems that seem as if they 're here to stay?
From Tomorrow
Is it a day in which
You want to run and hide;
Because of its anger,
Hoping and praying
To be relieved by the one born in a manger. Will it bring tears and all sorts of fears? All the time you're hoping your prayers are open to the Saviors ears, is it something to be despised,
Because of the schemes
That are there to your surprise.
Tomorrow
A day and time that must come to past, yet we know that today will never last.
A day in which the Sun will rise on those that are in the land of the living. Also they to are all for the giving.
Tomorrows
Are forever there's no changing; they have names just like you and I, not lasting forever they also die.
Tomorrow'
Some are cold, and some are wet, some bring risks causing you to bet.
Coming also in unawares, most surely with their own cares.

They've been around since the beginning of time; not only belonging
to others,
But also mine.
Tomorrows
Can be bright also being dark, not always being
A walk in the park.
Tomorrows
Can be sweet, also holding love.
Together growing wings they can fly away as a dove.
Will Tomorrows grow wings and fly away? Tell me are you sure to see
another Day?
TAD 5-27-03

Death

Death
Is it something?
That should cause fear?
Death
It comes our way
As if someone
Has hurled at us a spear.
Death
For sure must come to us all;
Death
Has been called many things;
But the main thing is the great fall.
Death
Can be frightening and sometimes very gory
Death
Is the end result of this life;
It is the end of the story.
Death
Also can come our way in many, many ways
Death
Knows our name and the number of our days.
Death will come it has no respect;
Death is like playing cards
With a loaded Deck.

Death, Death
Why do you hide?
You're at my door!
You just want to come inside.
One thing for sure I'll see you face to face;
I pray to God it won't be a disgrace.
Death
Is something I've known
Since I was a child.
Death
Told me it will come with a smile.
The life that we live can be long;
All so long as a country mile.
Death
In this world is not the end.
In all due actually;
Death
Is something that we must begin?
Death
Sometimes bring sorrow and pain
Thank God for Jesus
And the power that is in his name.
TAD 4-24-03

Does Life Wear You Down?

Does Life wear you down?
Causing you to wear a permanent frown?
The world does it seem cruel,
Playing games, using tricks,
That they call rules;
Leaving you wondering,
What's wrong, what's right?
Seeming like a never ending fight,
Things that you dread
Do they seem to last forever
And a night.
Does life wear you down?
Making you afraid to see another day,
Wondering how will it end,

Even though you forgot to pray;
Friends, do they turn their back
Leaving you alone?
Because of the way they say you act.
Life is it wearing you down
Filling you with days of so many tears.
Because of a mistake that you thought would
Last for years.
Compassing your heart with so much pain,
Within your days are nothing but rain.
You're nights being so dark
You cannot see,
Asking yourself about the future what will
It be? Do you sometimes ask yourself is there a
Place I can find to lay my head
And why must the streets be my bed
Does life wear you down?
Making your life seem like a joke
That hasn't been told, causing your youth
To change; before its time.
Making you feel alone
Although all and all giving you strength;
Letting you know;
All you have to do is be Bold.
TAD 5-27-03

Morning Flower

My Morning, Flower
Is beside me
And in my heart all the time;
I'm so glad she blossoms so pretty and all of her love is mine.
My Morning Flower
To me is more than life.
My Morning Flower
Is my mind, soul, body and spirit.
Thank God she's my wife.
Her love that she gives to me was
They're in the beginning;

The way we feel about each other—
Is strong, letting us know
With our togetherness;
There is no ending!
Morning Flower,
My Morning Flower her ways are soft, all so soft, tender and sweet,
Her warm, loving smile;
Sweeps me off of my feet.
My Flower,
My Morning Flower, she's always there meeting all of my wants and
needs, without her in my life; I know without a doubt my heart
would do nothing but bleed.
My Morning Flower,
Because of her in my life,
There is never any pain or guilt, without her my life would most
surely whither and wilt.
My Morning Flower
Will bloom and grow forever
And always;
For I know together
We both will see;
Many, many, days!
Morning Flower—

More Than Good

More than Good
Is what I want to be to you;
More than Good
Is what I want to do for you.
More than Good
Its how I feel;
When we're near each other
Feeling More than Good
Makes me never;
Want to be with another.
Your Love makes me feel
More than Good towards you;
Making me unable to refuse
Whatever you want me to do.

Wherever we may be
More than Good
I'll be to you;
So the whole world can see.
More than Good
Is what your love is to me,
Loving you forever
Never telling you never
Is how it will always be;
Forever and ever.
Life without end worlds away;
For God knows
That we'll be together everyday.
More than Good
Is how it is being together?
You and me
your smile lights up the night
that I may see.
That's the way its always been;
Your love makes me feel so good
it must be a sin.
Making love to you
is all I ever want to do;
its very sweet it drips;
like the mountains dew.
The aroma is so sweet,
it causes my body heat.
That's the way we are together;
it keeps us together
through all kinds of weather.

Fate

Is Fate taking you to a place
where you have never been?
Taking you from what you have been doing again and again.
Is Fate something that you feel you should fear?
Was it far away;
but now it seems all so near?

Portrait Of A Man

From Fate you can't run;
its something that must be done.
It was there
from the beginning of time;
not only your fate but also mine.
I once heard its greater than—
anything known.
It'll be around
when your life is completely gone!
Also its wisdom for all it knows;
a brooks stream of water
and the way it flows.
Fate is weak, also strong;
it's also the way of an angel's song.
Fate is something that seeks us all;
it's the summer,
spring, winter and fall.
Once small, once great, it's like the Seven seas and the great lakes.
Deep as an ocean, stronger than any love potion.
It can be peace in a storm,
it's there to keep you warm.
It has eyes,
often it's greatly despised.
Fate
It's cold, hot and warm,
also the way bees may swarm.
TAD 6-7-03

Inside Of A Storm

Inside of a Storm
is where dreams are born.
Although the darkness
tries to bring scorn.
There inside has always been light;
that must be sought
with all of your might.
The storm and in its midst
life can be found.
Building you up;

after being cast down.
Once inside the ways are rough;
often cold and very tough.
Fears that you feel are just to deceive;
trying to block the goals
that you must achieve.
Yet and still the waves will arise;
Although, to God this is no surprise.
Even though
it's not always cold;
the wisdom learned
Is as good as Gold.
There never seems to be any light;
this is just to show
life can be a fight.
One thing for sure
you must not be weak;
strength and power
is what you must seek.
On the other side are riches and wealth;
abundant life and goodness of health.
Out of the Storm
is the top of the Mountain;
rivers of living waters
flowing out of a golden fountain.
TAD 5-28-03

Life Is A Challenge

Life Is a Challenge
Not just for me.
But for all that is alive;
which is plain to see.
The challenges that we face each and everyday.
some of the test are so great
we fall to our knees
and pray they come
to make us stronger;
giving us wisdom

Portrait Of A Man

that our lives will last longer.
They come to us all in any season
spring, winter and fall.
Don't let the challenges
Wear you down;
Causing you sadness and a frown.
Sometimes putting on you
a large and heavy load;
Pressures unbelievable
that may cause you to explode.
Surely this life is
and has always been a challenge;
believe it yes or no,
it can also weight you down;
blind your mind leaving you aimless
with no where to go.
Everyday challenges come our way,
often turning our lives upside down;
but please don't loose your way.
Challenges of this life do they deceive;
causing you to feel alone
rejections come from those
you confide in
leaving you asking yourself
is this world really your home.
Everyone you seem to know;
thinks for you they know what's best.
And truly what your soul needs is rest.
Those of Low degree,
tell me how could this be?
has the world shaken you that much;
leaving you to believe the Father
His heart you cannot touch.
TAD 6-7-03

Heaven

Is Heaven only in a place
that you can't see?
Heaven is it on earth

also for you and me?
Is it in your heart
and part of the one you love?
Or Heaven is it only sent down
from the father
who sits high on the throne?
Far, Far above;
is it in the voice and actions
of one that is close to you?
Causing you to wonder
without this person;
what would you do?
Is it also in the smile of a friend
or someone you care for so dearly?
Was it in someone you miss
you all most new better only nearly?
Heaven
is it in your thoughts
that you want to share?
Although, you were unable to relate
because of fear
and in your heart there wasn't any care.
Did it come as a surprise?
your downfall it came to demise.
Coming also when days are cold
and the Sun is bright;
warming your heart
and shinning its soul loving light.
Touching your spirit feeling so good;
Putting a fire in your heart
like burning wood.
Heavenly feelings
are they sometimes in your body
often hard to contain;
as the blood you have
flowing through each and every vein.
Is it a place you go to all alone?
Letting you know
this world is not really your home.
Is this a land on the other side of the sky?

Where there's
always Howdy Hi and never Goodbye.
TAD 5-28-03

The Old Man

The Old Man
has dreams that reach beyond the stars;
The Old Man
and His wise tales will be one day strong,
stronger than iron Bars.
The Way of his wisdom
is far past understanding;
The Old Man lived
a long life that also was very demanding.
The Man that is Old
was foreseen before the day of his conception;
The Old Man is still keen and witty in his perception.
The strength in his body is that of a Lion;
His appearance is deceiving
He's still able to climb Mount Zion!
The Man that is Old
and the ways that he portray;
most surely establishes
that He is looking towards
an everlasting bright and Sunny day.
The Old Man that lives
the wisdom that is in his heart;
knows the value of life
and that he must do his part.
The Man himself has youth forever more,
The Old Man
is the same and
knows that God will open His door.
The Old Man
Himself knows where He must stand;
For in his hand is the key to the Promised Land.

The Old Man
Himself He fought a good fight;
Now once and for all He'll meet the Father of Lights.
TAD 4-25-03

Life Goes On

Are there times in your life
In which you wish that you could relive?
Only to find there was nothing there to
Receive or give.
If what could have been;
Had come into view;
Tell me, tell me,
What would be there for you to do?
Life Goes on
Time, It doesn't stop for no one,
No matter when or where
Time, about you it doesn't care.
What wasn't done will never be;
What must be will needs be.
That which hasn't been
Was never there;
Life Goes On
To what place tell me where;
Life would you really want it to stop?
That would not happen; would it not?
It goes to a place unknown;
Like a wonderer most surely it roams.
Life is like water over a waterfall;
Freely it flows to us all.
Life Goes On
In this world to and Fro;
Which way? Who's to know?
It often goes on and on;
From when to where;
It can't be seen.
It's thin as air,
Its effects are everywhere.

Wherever life takes you
That's where you'll be
Life for sure is not forever;
That's one thing everyone can see.
TAD 5-28-03

Diamonds Are Forever

Diamonds shine and glitter;
Brighter than Ice.
Harder than steal
More purer than Gold.
Diamonds are forever;
So I am told.
Diamonds are forever
Found deep down in the earth.
Diamonds
Are very expensive
Only God knows their true worth.
Diamonds
Are very strong;
They can make you happy and
Give you a heart-felt song.
Glitter and shine
Glitter and shine;
Diamonds
Their brilliance
Can make you drunk as wine.
Diamonds are Forever
Also they have their own soul,
Diamonds
Have a history and a story
That must be told.
Diamonds are
Like stars that
Hang in the skies
Diamonds are
The precious jewels
That God has for eyes.
Diamonds

Are our future
And also our past
Diamonds are Forever
One of the only things
That will eternally last
Diamonds are Forever
For a price unknown to man
Diamonds are Forever
More plentiful than all the Seas
And oceans and every grain of sand.
Forever Are Diamonds
In lives and worlds to come
Diamonds I believe Are Forever
also in worlds and planets all around the Sun.
Diamonds are Forever.

Time

Who's to know the value of time?
Time
Moves on it waits for no one.
Time
Does it belong to you or me?
Is it something that will always be?
Time
Itself cannot be seen,
Its effects sometimes are cruel and mean.
Time
Will always past, nothing,
Nothing in the world will ever last.
It's giving to us all;
It changes from spring, winter, and summer to fall.
Time
It can't be bought; sometimes for this wars are fought.
Time
Is life, also death, it can be a person's breath.
Taking you sometimes to places unknown;
Able also to give you a greater home.
Going slow, going fast,

most surely it will past.
Time
It brings the day, it brings the night.
Endurance of it you'll find is a fight.
It causes us all to age,
Its ways are like a book with an eternal page.
Time
Knows all, for all is time,
It was in the beginning and after the fall.
Although, it is like a revolving door,
It is something of which we want more and more.
It has the wisdom of many ages;
Like that of a book with many pages,
It's like a race it tells who will last;
Also letting us know for sure all will past.
Time
As if a cloud hanging over your head,
Time will be there
Waiting for you on your deathbed.
TAD 5-28-03

Risking Your Life

Is something in your life so important
That you may be willing to die?
Tell Me!
Can this substance
Enrich your well-being?
Or is just one big Lie?
Risking Your Life
Life itself is always full of risks
This is something everyone knows.
The Risks of Life
Should not be followed
Wherever the wind blows!
Risking Of Your Life
Is something that must be done;
At one time or another, in life itself you should never
have to depend on and put your trust in a brother.
While risking your life

You must surely realize you'll stand alone,
Once this is accomplished;
This world you'll feel
Is no longer your home!
Nothing ventured, Nothing Gained!
This is a fact that always was just like a peach
And all of its fuzz.
Life itself is full of many risks; they spin around and around like a
spinning disk.
TAD 4-29-03

Jesus Is Our Father

Jesus Is Our Father
Each and every hour.
All is in His hands,
Especially all the power.
His ways are right;
For His children;
He will always fight.
His ways are near;
Close to your heart;
Keeps His love dear.
When He leads
There's never any fear.
He loves us all so much;
Our lives He's sure to touch.
With His supernatural grace.
It comforts us in this race.
From the beginning
He was foretold;
Before time He was there,
Older that old;
Pure as gold.
Freedom in life is what He gives;
For abundantly we may live.
Much more than divine,
His spirit is for all;
not just mine.

Portrait Of A Man

Always strong and bold;
His life must be told.
The Sun is always shinning bright,
within that way
there's never any night.
Although only to those
who accept His will,
others belong to the dark
who's way is to kill.
The fight is between the two,
what will you decide to do?
Life belongs to God,
His judgments
are quick as a lightening Rod.
His ways were sent to the earth;
in the form of a virgin birth.
Being the master of light;
casting the enemy out
with hardly a fight.
TAD 5-28-03

[Shame]

Is shame something
that you fear most?
does it rob you—
and threaten you;
making you feel like a ghost?
Shame
Is it something that can be seen?
Shame
Is it always disgraceful?
Sometimes tasteless
and always unclean?
Shame
Does it make you want
To cover your face?
Find what's inside of yourself;
and establish your own place.

Ted Alan Dyer

Shame
Is something
that will lead you to your grave
Shame
Guilt and Pride
will make you turn your back
On life—
even though you are saved!
Shame
Itself has no strength within;
Its power is worthless
Shame
Is Sin!
Shame
is conceived by not following through;
Shame
is derived sometimes from nothing to do!
The mind becomes idle
and so does the heart—
Then comes;
Shame
doing its Part!
Shame
Itself is something to be feared;
being of the Father—
That's not how you were reared!
The world in which we live
is full of so much!
Shame
Everything is done in the devils name!
Thank God!
That we are not related—
Fighting Fire with Fire;
That's the way to go,
That's a trick of the devil don't you know.

Shame
quiet as a cemetery,
In the middle of the night.
You can't even hear a pin drop
Shame it's just one big fight.
TAD 4-23-03

Destiny

Is Destiny the same as fate?
Of course they both lead to the same road
In which you take.
Both lead to the same place;
Destiny
Sometimes is a never ending Race.
Most often at the end of life;
also it comes with a price.
Although it can be seen and felt;
having the power to touch your heart
making you melt.
Also a place, which can bring sorrow;
with Destiny—
Sometimes there's no tomorrow.
Yet and still it can bring years of wealth;
even happiness and goodness of health.
The end result is everything
that was ever conceived.
Its reality is for sure it can only be received.
Destiny
itself can be deep as a cave,
most surely your last breath and the grave.
Destiny
is the truth, also the lie,
also something that will never die.
It was there when nothing else was,
also the bees and the way they buzz..
The flowers and the way they grow;
the winter months and all of its snow.

Destiny
is the moon, stars and all the planets,
its tough, strong, hard as granite.
Destiny
Is the song of a chirping bird,
often seen but seldom heard.
Also looking for a place in your mind,
seeking wisdom—
that your sure to find.
TAD 5-28-03

Life Is A Spirit

Life Is A Spirit
That consist thereof;
Life is not only a spirit;
but all that is within
has their own portion of Love.
Trust is a thing far;
So very far in the past;
Most of all nothing in this life
will ever last.
Trust also is for those
who are only willing to believe!
Trusting in God
Your problems He will relieve.
Life Is A Spirit
Something so mysterious
that it can not be conceived
The Spirit was sent to keep you safe;
Does the Spirit have a body,
Or does the spirit have a soul
or is the spirit one of a kind that came from a story foretold?
The Spirit
Is everlasting to its life there is no end;
Life Is A Spirit
The Spirit itself also can be your closest friend.
The Spirit
Is here to lead, protect and to Guide

From the Spirit Of Life
It is most impossible for anyone to hide!
The Spirit
Is there to take away fear;
The Spirit
whispers all so gently in my ear
Often telling me the things it feels;
that I should know,
But most of all telling Me
Which way that I should go.
Life Is A Spirit
The Spirit
Itself always does its Part;
Just listen Closely—
the spirits home is in your heart!
The Spirit
Itself is larger than a Giant;
Also very Bold and over flowing
with courage Also full of power
and very defiant.
Life is a Spirit 4-17-03

Eternity

Eternity, is it a place that can't be seen:
With the naked eye?
If it was, we would never have to die.
Also it can bring eternal pain;
Sometimes in this place
Hell fire it rains.
It for sure can be eternal bliss;
who really knows if a mark you missed?
A place I believe that's far, far away;
also closer than a everlasting day.
With you who will it be spent?
Time now to you it was lent.
It belongs to God and Him Alone
For this is His Eternal Home
His Throne sits high and up above;
He stepped out on nothing but Love.

It has no time, neither yours nor mine.
In the midst of nothingness it hangs out in space;
to reach there would be an everlasting race.
The Universe belongs to eternity and all creation;
because of that we must be in relation.
Must it be seen in a different shade of light;
Within this place
Is there any substance;
or wars to fight?
Or should it be sought with all your might?

The Ways Of The Day

The Day is a time to be;
Sunny and bright
The sun is so cheerful there's no need to fight.
The Ways Of The Day
will make you smile;
Your heart will be so happy;
You could run a country mile.
The fragrance of the Day fresh and sweet
the cool summer breeze
sweeps through the streets.
The skies are so blue;
it beckons to you.
On top of the sky
there are many, many,
worlds that can't be seen.
There so far away they make you wonder;
Do you become afraid;
when there's lightening
and thunder?
The Ways Of The Day
when the sun is hot
and the heat makes you perspire;
throughout the days do you live your desires.
Are their riches to be earned
and lessons to be learned.

When the day begins to end
and the twilight dawn has arrived;
have you prepared for the dark
in order to survive.
The Ways Of The Day
have a spirit within itself;
there's magic in the air—
obtain it if you Dare.
Daytime,
so up comes the sun out of the east,
Down it goes in the west;
did you remember throughout the day
to always, always give it your best?
TAD 4-19-03

The Ways Of The Night

The Ways Of The Night;
are they wrong or right?
Are the nights long
and cold demanding
nothing but a fight?
The Ways Of The Night
are they the same as the Day?
Or are they harder to find
than a needle-in a bail of hay?
Night Ways
Do they seem hard,
rough and cruel?
The Ways Of The Night
sometimes mean death;
The Night Air
can also take your breath.
The Ways Of The Night
is longer than the Day;
The Nights
Are so dark you can't see your face.
To become lost in the dark
would be such a disgrace!

The Ways Of The Night
To fear the dark
would be more than a shame
maybe that's why the blind—
carries a cane.
The Night! The Night!
sometimes may bring fears
to others—nothing but tears!
But most of all when the morning comes
they'll be nothing but cheers;
The Way Of The Night
can be tough and rough;
hard and cruel;
chilling your soul
Making its own rules.
TAD 6-7-03

The Power Of The Sword

The Sword is swift;
It cuts like a knife.
The way of the sword
Is a hell of a fight.
The power of the sword
Is in your mind.
The power of the mind
Is one of a kind.
The sword and the mind
They both intertwine.
They act as one something to be reckoned;
Their actions are quick as a second.
Their power is great,
Still yet to be known.
The swords power will take you home.
The swords power is in your hand,
It will also make you stand.
Also it is strong as can be;
The sword will open your eyes
And make you see.

All so quick, all so fast,
It can take your life
And cause you to past.
Strong, strong and bold.
The sword keeps you warm
When it's Ice Cold.
It's also there to do its part;
Looking deep within your heart.
The will of the sword is also zealous;
Full of fire and very jealous.
Very quick very sharp,
It also plays music like a harp.
Although sometimes very mean,
Cutting deep down in between.
It is powerful strong as a hex,
Your spirit and soul it will not vex.
The way of the world is all so cold;
It also protects so stand Bold.
You'll stand real tall just like a king
Sword in hand even with wings.
Wishful thinking can be bright as the Sun;
With a sword from Dreams you'll never run.
Its power is great, and always near,
Its power is something you should respect and fear.
The way of itself is very unknown and deep
Letting you see that others are weak.
TAD 6-6-03

Mind Of A Child

The Mind Of A Child
Sees within our hearts
A Childs mind has an eye of intelligence;
That's smarter than smart.
The Mind Of A Child
Is more than brilliant
Yet and still A Childs mind is always resilience
A Childs Mind
Has its own way of thinking;
God at our little ones

He's always winking;
The Mind Of A Child
Is in everyone young and old
The Value of their mind
Is as good as gold.
Inside of their mind is a
Spiritual eye;
One thing for sure the child inside will never die.
The Mind Of A Child
Is like a dream that flies away on a bright and sunny day;
A Childs mind is full of work
And also play
The Mind Of A Child
Is everywhere at the same time
A Childs Mind
Ripens with age
Just like the purest of wine
Inside Of A Childs Mind
Are dreams and wishes for everyone?
A Childs Mind
Has a golden key
That is given by God
That unlocks a Golden Door
The Mind Of A Child
Is richer than Heaven
And all the treasure thereof
One thing for sure
The Mind Of A Child
And God the Father are one of a kind
Straight from His throne better
Known as Love.
TAD 4-25-03

Dreams

The life that we live
Is it just a Dream?
Tell Me?
Who's in control?

And why are we full of schemes?
Dreams
The world in which we
Live is it just one big joke;
Sometimes causing our Dreams to—
Go up in smoke!
Dreams
Each dream is different;
Just like the days of the week.
Tell Me?
Within your dreams;
What is it that you seek?
Dreams
They all can be interpreted
Just like what's two and two.
Dreams
They all have meanings
Just like the lives we live;
Some Dreams
Tell us to receive;
But it is better to give.
Dreams
They never deceive
Dreams
Can be more real
Than reality!
Dreams
Sometimes are—
Our true personality!
Dreams
They're our thoughts
And desires;
Dreams
Themselves can be—
Burning fires!
Dreams
Are higher than
The highest mountain
Dreams
Can be love flowing

Ted Alan Dyer

From a fountain.
Dreams
Are in our hearts
And we see them
With our eyes;
Dreams
And the act of dreaming
Is something
We shouldn't despise!
Dreams
Come to us as a cloud
That floats through the air;
Dreams
Can be an inspiration
When no one cares.

Forever Day

Forever Day
When the long nights cease
And morning sunlight
Is on its way;
Tell Me? In this life
Will it ever be forever day?
The eyes of the day follow us all
Always letting us know that the night will call!
Beckoning to all—
That is in the land of the living
Showing us the moonlight
And the way of it's giving!
Never in this land
Will it remain forever day;
For sure this will be
In the land to which we pray!
Forever Day
Always bright this land
Is enlightened
By the Father of lights!

Forever Day
This way is clear and it has
Always been sent down
To the earth to cleanse our sins.
Daytime Forever
Sounds to good to really be true
If it was so in this world
What would you do?
Day and night
Seems as if it will always be;
Which do you choose?
Thank God!
It's not up to thee.
Creatures of the day is
How we were foreseen
Then came the Prince Of Darkness;
Surely his way is mean.
From him we were redeemed
And believe me it was with a fight,
Bought by the Father and his marvelous light.

Lonely Heart

Lonely Heart
Her heart is so lonely;
It turns me blue
Tell Me? Tell Me?
What shall I do?
The way that I'll take
I hope and pray;
Blue Lonely Hearts
Will go away!
A heart that is full of pain;
They're just like
The bright sunny days
That are full of rain!
Trying to deceive and
Keeping me in despair,
Leaving me helpless
And realizing all of my shame.

Yet and still
Her blue lonely heart
Sees my soul
It looks deep within
To a story that should be told.
Blue Lonely Hearts
Seem to have a mind of their own
Looking for sadness
That they may call their home.
A Blue lonely heart
Will make you soft and weak;
You must be strong
To avoid the devil's temptations You'll seek!
Lonely Hearts
That are blue and often full of fears
The pain within may cause many of tears
Hearts blue
And lonely sometimes burn with fire
They also can be consumed with an evil desire,
The ways of the heart are greatly unknown
Whither thou goest or where is their home!
Lonely Heart

Truth

Truth
Is it something
That we must learn
Truth
Must be instilled within us or we will most certainly in hell burn.
Truth
And its substance was implanted;
Within the earth
A gift from God to man to
See if we could find its worth.
Truth
Should be valued more than the most precious of stones
Truth should be an unquenchable fire burning
Inside of your bones

Truth has always been the beginning and the end
Truth
Actually was meant to be your closes friend.
Truth
And that which is true is larger than large
Truth
Itself has more
Authority than an army and each and every serge.
Truth
Is like a doctor and the medicine
He gives us to take
Without Truth
In your life is like being bitten by a poisonous snake
Without this substance life is truly in vain
Truth
And darkness for sure is just not the same
Truth
Has a price that must be bought;
Behind Truth
There's a lesson to be taught.
Truth
Is always first and never last
Although for some its a very hard task.
Truth
Is like a Rod-That's sent
To correct!
Truth
Is more valuable than an exceedingly large check.

Wings Of The Night

On The Wings of the night
Is where I've always
Longed to take Flight.
The wings of the night have always been my home
High above the stars is where I'll forever roam.
The Wings Of The Night
Are soft and smooth
They'll take me
To my Heavenly Home

That's where I'll move
The Wings Of The Night
Are there to be free
Flying so high for all to see.
On The Wings Of The Night
There's power unknown
On a cushion of air is where they belong
Night Wings
Fly high, higher than high,
Taking me to a land
Where there's never a goodbye.
Wings Of The Night
Are inside of your heart
Touching your soul and spirit
Allowing God to do His part.
The peace of the Wings
Are worth more than gold
Climbing higher than the mountains
Which were ordained
Before times of old
Wings Of The Night
Will take you away from this world and all of its shame.
With The Wings Of The Night
You can fly away as in a dream
And never come back
Or so it seems
The Wings Of The Night
They fly swift and fast
The flight of
The Night Wings
Will forever last
Wings Of The Night

Years

How many
Years
May pass you by
Before you decide

To find yourself?
Throughout the decades
Did you get lost?
Seeking for fame and wealth?
Years
While finding your real self
did you realize that once found
it was the greatest
thing that could be,
Although all the time you find yourself wondering
Why before this time yourself you could not see.
Years
They come and go to us all
sometimes slow but often fast
Years
They change our lives in different ways
Even though the future and the past
will most often clash.
Passing away quick as a light with a flash.
Days change to weeks,
weeks, changes to months
and months turns to years,
sometimes wounding us
and bringing tears.
The time of the years
will heal our pain,
only in the Father
and His Holy Name.

Strangers In The Night

Strangers In The Night
is that how your life seems to be
not knowing who's sincere
but always trying to see.
Passing strangers within the night
are they really strangers or
do we just need a light.
Strangers and Friends are they both the same
or are they lost in the dark seeking a name

Strangers found in the night
Do we know
Who they really are?
Do they come from near?
Or from away
All so very far
Within the night
Are there things
That should be feared?
Or from the time of our youth
Is that how we were reared?
Within itself
Are their times to hold dear?
Especially the rest we get
And the quietness we hear
Strangers within the Night
Do they pass one another?
With hardly a care,
Forming dreams in their mind
seems to be only a dare.
Without the day there's no night
Without night there's no day;
they both need each other
Like a child needs a Father and a mother.
Strangers In The Night
Are the Best of friends
There only need is
A shoulder to lend.
Strangers In The Night
Come in many colors, shapes and sizes;
Often wearing mask and disguises
From where did they come?
To where will they go?
What is their purpose?
Tell Me?
Who is there that really knows?
TAD 6-7-03

Words Can Kill

If some of the words we speak
—Could kill; Tell Me?
How many people,
Would be inflicted
And become ill?
Whose heart would be pierced?
Through once known to us
What could we do?
Spoken words
Cannot be reclaimed
A bridled tongue;
Can't cause harm,
Wound and maim.
Destroying the spirit,
mind and soul;
Leaving pain inside
As a black empty hole
They soften our spirit
harden our soul!
Telling a story
that shouldn't be told
If words could kill!
Would anyone be left within
this Planet?
Or would their names be inscribed;
In marble and granite.
From this was there
A void giving?
Does it make hopeless
Any thought of living
and going on with life?
Because of tension and strife.
Strife wasn't intended
To invade our lives;
Its venom is deadly,
Cruel and sharp as a knife.

Words that could kill
Our pride it will degrade;
Exploding within our souls just like a grenade.

Respect

Respect is something that should be earned not learned;
Respect
Gratifies the heart, mind, body and soul.
Respect
Has been around since the beginning of time,
There's nothing new about it
Respect
Is older than old.
It's always warm
And never cold.
Respect
Has always been the
Way to live.
Respect
It's never selfish always willing to give.
Respect
Is love it never fails
Respect
Is of the father,
Maybe because of this and its lack of
The Son was driven through with nails.
Respect
It comes from the heart a very essential need,
Without this substance all about you would bleed.
Respect
Itself always comes from within
It's not haunty,
And full of pride
No Respect
Is the worst level of sins.
It's gained by the desire to survive.

Respect
Dwells in each and everyone of us,
it's given to guide.
Respect
Doesn't judge according
to what one thinks.
Respect
makes you wonder why
the ship that your own
Doesn't sink.
Respect
One's self,
Specially in the mist of a storm,
Because the times change
Eventually it will get warm.
TAD 7-18-03 Fri. 4:40 p.m.

Mid-Night Skies

Mid-Night Skies, Skies of the night;
Skies always you're filled with stars
That illuminates my life.
Mid-Night Skies, Skies of the night;
Looking as if you're made of dreams
Within you I want to take a flight.
Mid-Night Skies, Mid-Night Dreams
Both are the same or so it seems,
Skies of Mid-Night
Dreams, filled with stars for Gemstones,
Lined with Golden seams.
Mid-Night Skies, Mid-Night Dreams
Both are the same or so it seems.
Mid-Night Dreams, Mid-Night Dreams
Please stay forever
Don't fly away with invisible wings.
Skies of the Dark misty nights;
Filling my heart with all so much intrigue,
Compelling my spirit to be in the midst of you,
Mid-Night Skies, Mid-Night Skies
Reminding me of my second home;

Without you what would I do?
Although you fade away all too soon,
Mid-Night Skies, Mid-Night Skies
I love the glory of your spirit
Also the glowing of your moon.
Mid-Night Moon Rays
Shinning upon the earth
All the while it is spinning around,
Casting its shadow
Upon all making them feel heaven bound.
Mid-Night Star filled with Dreams;
Mid-Night Skies, Mid-Night Skies
Takes me away form a world filled with schemes.
TAD 7-16-03 Tues. 1:18 am

When The Moon Is Full

When the Moon Is Full
And all is dark, are there feelings
That you feel if walking in the park?
And all that is shinning
are the rays of the moon,
Now you're wondering
If you will ever see high noon.
The weeds are moving,
Bushes shaking,
You find yourself running,
And your heart is breaking.
Trembling and frantic
Is all you know,
You're blowing with the wind
Wherever it goes.
Running so fast
You're loosing your breath,
When you look back
All you see is Mr. Death.
The fear inside
Is trying to take over
You're moving so fast

Portrait Of A Man

Just like a land rover;
Tripping and Stumbling
All the way through;
If this is not a dream
What will you do?
Falling on your face
Would be such a shame,
You'd probably die laughing
But this is not a game.
Afraid of dying
You start to curse,
all you can think of is riding in a Hearst.
You hear something growling sounding like
Roof, Roof,
You realize you're
In a cemetery
Could this be a werewolf.
Footsteps approaching
Is all you can hear,
Paralyzed within and gripped by fear.
No need to fight,
no need to fuss,
Your biggest fear is
getting hit by a bus.
TAD 6-30-03 11:15 pm

Love In The Shade

Making Love in the Shade
Can be steamy and hot,
Sweet as can be
Just find the right spot.
Making Love in the shade
Should it really be this way?
Shouldn't it be under
The hot, hot burning Sun;
Becoming as one
Each and every day?
Desire is hot within a heart, soul, body and mind,
It gives life it's one of a kind.

I prayed to God for this heavenly delight
Never in my wildest dreams
Would I have thought
it would be;
Such a hell of a fight!
Had I only known the pleasures it would bring,
Love in the shade
Would be an everyday thing.
For something so pure
I would surely die,
All I desire is too be deep inside.
Love making in the shade
Is like two candles
Burning in the night,
They melt themselves down together without a fight.
Love the shade
And under the hot blazing Sun,
Is both hot and cool by all this should be done.
Making love in the shade
With a misty warm breeze,
Relaxes your mind and puts your soul at ease.
Love In The Shade
Is chilling to the spirit when the sun goes down,
Love in the shadows
makes the world go around;
Hot, cold, cool or warm.
Love in the shade
Is sweet as honey
around which the honey bees may swarm.
TAD 7-20-03 Sun. 7:00 pm

Night Visions

Night can bring visions
that come and go
In the twinkling of an eye.
Night Visions
Can prolong your days
That death may not be as nigh.

Also, able to appear in the way seem; that in the midst of the day,
as a warning that you might not go astray.
Night Visions
seem to have a way of getting your attention,
Distracting harm that might come;
It's here for prevention.
Visions seen in the Night,
Visions within the Day,
Not only can come to me,
But also to lead your way.
Night Visions
Most likely have a will
Of their own,
Seeking and wondering for a soul
To which they can call home.
The ability to see future
Events would be called
The greatest lie ever told;
It's only given to a hand
Full bought and sold.
Visual perception of things
That's yet to occur,
Is this reality?
Or is it just a blur?
Night Visions
Are they really what they seem?
Is it your spirit
That they're here for?
Coming to redeem!

Future Life

Future Life
Who's to know what the future may bring?
Will it bring fire and Brimstone?
Or the way angels may sing.
Future Life,
What is this thing that beckons to us all?
It comes in many forms for sure it calls.
Life in the future is like passing through

Corridors, and halls by most it cannot
Be perceived, yet and still to the end is the fall.
Futuristic, living may seem like
Reality, it's how life was formed in all due actuality.
Future Life
Where does it lead, from where did it come?
One thing for sure,
From it you cannot run.
Life within the future
Is the same as the past;
Both fades away none will last.
Future Life
Life within the future
What is there
That's for sure to occur
If it was at all possible
Would you try and deter?
Going straight ahead
With the master plan;
Giving it all to God and his outstretched hands.
Life within this sphere will out live us all;
Day by day, year by year.
TAD 7-18-03 Fri. 5:04 am

Momentum

Gaining Momentum
Within life can be like
A down hill battle,
Momentum
In excess
Will shake some
And make their cage rattle.
Momentum
Itself is a powerful force,
If you don't believe me
Find another source.
Momentum
Itself is force gained,

Portrait Of A Man

Thrusting, pushing through
the world wanting to make a name!
Momentum
Can travel faster
Than the speed of light!
Momentum
Should be sought after
With all your might!
Forced gained often renamed!
Momentum
Drives within also it can maim.
Down hill speed can be dangerous,
So take heed!
Gaining Momentum
Within this life gains a source of comfort;
When the world is cold as Ice!
Passing through life attracting what's needed,
Seems as if it's something in which all has pleaded.
Momentum
Gained, is ventured earned,
All through life
There are lessons to be learned.
Centrifugal forces
Is derived from life itself
Making one wise.

A Woman's' Romance

A Woman's' Romance
Can be witty and deceptive,
Although you must remain
keen and perceptive.
Her Romance that she gives
It's full of pride and distinction,
It's always on time
There will never be any extinction.
A woman is full of desire
and Romance
Her heart has nothing
but secrets

And emotional stances.
Standing always for what she needs and feels
Driven by her emotions her heart and her will.
A Woman's Romance
Is deep as the center of the earth,
Looking for a strong man to find it's worth!
The Romance Of a Woman
Should always be cherished,
Without it for sure I would perish.
Romancing a Woman
Seems to be a great, great, need
It nourishes the spirit and soul
The importance is devastating
So please take heed.
A Woman's Romance
Was thrust within the earth
Since the beginning of time,
meant for those for whom it could find.
Love and making Romance
Is a game that the whole world loves to play?
Each and everything was conceived this way.
TAD 7-14-03 Mon. 6:34 pm

Deserts Of Life

Is there a drought in your life
That just won't go away?
Times seem to be so hard
All you can do is fall on your knees and pray!
The Deserts Of Life
Can always be overtaken,
Only seek God
And your dreams
Will be awaken!
They have not come
as a deceiver
Testing your faith,
Demanding courage
Showing that you must always be a believer.

Portrait Of A Man

Desert lands within
The life we live,
Gives us the strength we need to survive storms,
Humble ourselves,
Open our hearts to receive and give.
Deserts Of Life
Purifies our soul, shines bright,
Brighter than the brightest of lights,
Bringing us the power we need to fight.
Dry lands and droughts
Opens to you the doors of others,
Letting you know that your not alone
and that God's will
The earth it will cover.
The wisdom and knowledge it brings,
makes life worth living
And a happy song you will always sing.
Teaching us not to despise
The hardships of life,
All can be overcome
Especially all of it's strife.
Deserts OF Life
And hardships all in the same,
Which seems to be a never-ending game.
But God came to revenge.
TAD 7-13-03 Sun. 11:34 p.m.

Will The Light Always Shine?

Will the light always shine?
Will every day be sunny and bright?
Just keep on living
And you'll discover—
That life is a never ending fight!
Holding on seems sometimes so very hard to do,
With God in your life;
For sure He will always bring you through.
Will the Light Always Shine?
The answer depends on you
and only you!

The Will that you display, show your belief;
Then ask yourself are sunny skies always blue.
If there was a time
When the light within
did not shine?
More than likely
It was the enemy
Trying to keep you behind.
Pushing his way into your soul,
Spirit and mind, keeping you in the dark he only wants to blind.
He himself is always there sifting your breath;
His only way is the grave and death.
Will the Light Always Shine?
Always shinning but not on you only!
More filling than the food
At your table.
Its glowing gives confidence and the ability to do all things there's no
doubt you're able. The light will always shine coming from above,
From the Father of Lights
The Father Of Love.
TAD 7-14-03 Mon. 12:08 am

Roads Of Our Lives

The Roads of Our Lives
Are always twisting and turning,
Sometimes bringing doubts, fears, and confusion;
Giving wisdom worth learning.
The Roads Of Our Lives
Leads to many places unknown;
Taking us often all so very far from home.
Sometimes leaving us stranded!
Not knowing which way to go,
Without a friend in the world there's—
Not anyone you know!
The Roads Of Our Lives
Can take us to an end
That is dead;
Giving us a future

In which all of us dread!
Roads can take you
Near or far,
Causing pain, devastating our lives,
Leaving us in fear,
And our bodies to be scared.
The Roads Of Our Lives
Takes us over mountains, hills,
and through tunnels,
Consuming us as a vacuum
Within a cloud of funnels.
Some lead to everlasting life!
And some to destruction!
Build your life on the straight and narrow
And then start construction!
At the cross roads of life
An important choice should be made,
just remember for this
Jesus Christ,
down his life was laid.
TAD 7-14-03 Mon. 1:30 am

Candles In The Night

Candles In The Night
Are like a lamp unto my soul;
within this light lives are bought
And lives are sold.
It's better to look into a candle
then curse the dark;
If this were not true;
then the devil would find his mark!
Candles In The Night
Can be brighter than the brightest
Watch tower upon the ocean,
Before the flickering of one candle
Can save a soul
In the moment of a notion.
Candles In the Night
Can come as death

With a smile on his face,
trying to out run this light
With a never ending race.
Sometimes within the night
candles may show you the way,
open the door;
To the newness of another day.
TAD 7-14-03 Mon. 3:36 am

Leaves Blowing In The Wind

The leaves of the trees blowing within the wind, Whispers gently to
my spirit
That a kind word they may lend.
Leaves Blowing In The Wind
Sounds as if their singing a spiritual hymn;
Comforting my spirit and mind,
Very softly leaving me to wonder
What are they seeking to find?
The Blowing Of The Leaves
Seems to caress the night air,
Calming me within easing each and every care.
Night breeze Blowing through the Leaves
Without a reason without a Dare.;
Smooth as silky Angel's hair.
Leaves swaying within winds of the night'
They swing together without a fuss or fight.
Floating and hanging on a branch
and stem, once and again
Sounding like a hymn.
Blowing Leaves seems to have a mind of their own;
Mostly coming alive at night
Hiding within their home.
Keeping themselves from the light;
Loving the night
With more than all of their might.
On occasions one may break off
And float away on a cushion of air
Unseen to the naked eye,

Finding a place to rest;
That's wherever they, may lye.
Often with seeds within the ground, it falls;
Cycle goes around and around
that after years and years,
it may grow big and tall!
TAD 7-16-03 Wed. 5:25pm

The Pressures Of Life

The Pressures of this Life
In which we live,
blinds our hearts and minds
Making us only want to
receive and never give.
The Pressures of Living
Often casting us down,
seeming like a raging sea
Causing us to nearly drawn.
Being tossed too and fro.
Hiding the light
blinding us with the snow;
destroying our lives
with what we don't know!
Leaves us wandering
With no where to go!
The Pressures Of Life
Will roll you over and around
turn you around
sometimes smother your life
without a sound.
Tossed aside as unwanted trash;
The Pressures Of This Life
Will drain you and steal all of your cash.
Pressures and the reasons why;
Will boggle the mind until you die!
Life and Its Pressures
Were brought about by lies and deceptions!
Which could have been prevented
By will power;

Saying no which is rejection!
TAD 7-18-03 8:10 pm

Mother's Day
(1923-1985)

Mother's Day, Mother's day
It seems to have grown wings
and flew all so far away.
Mother's Day, Mother's Day
Is there really such a thing?
Why, Oh why did it come with wings?
Seeming so lost and sometimes confused,
Why Oh why was mother's used?
Aches and Pains are more than many,
The cruelness of life is very plenty.
Living is cruel, crueler than cold,
or so it seems
Just keep getting old!
The oldness of life will soon pass away;
Allowing the sun to shine each and everyday.
A world so free and full of peace,
Anger has ceased, and there are no evil beast!
Worlds away far beyond the stars
A land of more than plenty, much farther than mars.
Far beyond the solar system
In which we live,
Free from God just accept
His Son this is something He Freely gives.
Mother's Day, Mother's Day
A gift from God
My poor old mom
Died on Mother's Day
Tell me do you think this was odd?
What more can you ask for a suffering soul,
So we all know life can be cold!!
TAD 7-7-03 10:20 pm

Wounds Of Life

Has Life wounded you so much—
That the pain is sometimes hard to bear?
The world is all so cold it seems no one cares!
Wounds Of Life
Tries to tear you down,
Destroy your faith and hope
Causing you to wear an everlasting frown.
Wounds of Life
Can pierce you through
Leaving scars that will
Last forever,
Causing you to ask yourself;
What in the world must I do?
Wounded and hurt torn asunder,
Feeling as if you've been struck
By thunder and lightning.
Within the days of thy youth
Wounds went unknown lying dormant
Until you become grown;
Scared, wounded beat down by the world
And its ways,
Although the wounds of life
Should by no means number your days.
Life and its worlds can fill you with anger,
and desolation,
Never allowing the promise of consultation.
Wounded and scorned
by all those that are around,
did you really think they would try
to keep your down?
Wounded, torn and bothered
This truly show you what really mattered.
Wounded in battle,
Scared for life,
does the sword really cut
like a two way knife?
TAD 7-18-03 Fri. 10:56 pm

Life

Life
What is this thing that is given so freely to all?
We all know it continued after the fall.
Life
Was it only meant to be taken in stride?
I once heard it said, it is only filled with pride.
Life
And in it of course are many of unknown ventures, some are comical
like a glass of dentures.
Also it can have many of troubles and woes,
people that can't be trusted
what else only God knows?
Living, a long and happy Life
Is something that everyone craves.
But the only way to receive the next life
Is through Christ!
He is the Only one that saves!
Life
We all know can be hard
cruel and sometimes not nice,
also mean and cold as Ice!
Was it really meant for everyone
With breath to breathe?
Or does most people have a trick up their sleeve.
The spirit of life affects us all,
no matter how large, big, fat, slim or tall.
Life
Has a road that comes to an end!
And the other side is a door;
When you get there
Will you be able to go straight in?
Life
Can be hell and heaven right here on earth;
find your value
For you must find its true worth!
The will of life
Only the strong can survive,
wisdom and Boldness

Will surely keep you alive.
TAD 6-26-03 11:15 pm

Subliminal Perception

Beyond the threshold of conscious perception
leaves some to seek reasons for believing;
Lying dormant within the soul and mind seeking the most brilliant of
thoughts it's always trying to find.
Thoughts and ambitions being brought to life,
cutting through the world as a sharpened knife.
Conscious perception is that which we see and perceive;
Although some things in life are hard to believe!
Pain and suffering
Is it all in the mind?
Beyond conscious perception should be sought after
Just like lost and find.
We ourselves are a five fold being;
We're only designed to believe what we are seeing.
conscious perception involves strength within the mind unknown to
man and the lives in the land;
More vast and plentiful than all the seas.
Along with each and every grain of sand.
Things not yet perceived why must this be so hard to believe?
We all come this way
For that's how we were conceived.
Believe without seeing is the greatest gift of all;
Had this occurred we would not had experienced the Great fall.
TAD 7-18-03 Fr. 11:20 pm

Cotton Tail

Cotton Tail, Cotton Tail
From where did you come?
And where are you going?
Cotton Tail, Cotton Tail
Every time I look
You seem to be growing.
Friendly and peaceful

Is the way you always are,
Even within the distance glances
No matter how far.
Your fur is full of many colors
With the wilderness
You easily blend.
Your freedom
Is so alluring to me
Will some of it, you lend?
Cotton Tail, Cotton Tail
You seem as if
You never have a care;
Making your home in the darkness and light
No matter when nor where!
Quiet as can be
Out of nowhere
You seem to come,
You're just like a free spirit
With you
I just want to have fun!
You remind me of a friend I've
always known;
You light up my life,
Please come into my home.
Cotton Tail, Cotton Tail
Tell me where is it that you hide?
Day to Day,
Night to Night,
you take it all in stride.
From me I wish you would not fear.
Cotton Tail
You make your home,
My home something I hold dear.
Cotton Tail, Cotton Tail
Within the forest, you live and hide, making me want to follow you
and be by your side.
TAD 7-13-03 Sun. 11:58 pm

The Pressures Of Life

The Pressures of this Life,
In which we live;
Binds our hearts,
Making us only want to receive
and never give.
Taking away from us the respect
That we should have for one another,
Which includes a friend, sister,
Brother, father or mother!
Life and its Pressures
Will take away your will to survive;
Causing you pain
Making you want to do nothing,
but hide!
The Pressures Of Living
Tries to keep you down;'
Without feelings of nothing
but despair
and desolation,
Taking away from you
Any form of consultation.
The Pressures Of Life
Will steal your soul;
Offer it to the devil
For silver and Gold!
Also, causing a lot to go astray
From what goodness
They were raised to believe;
Seeking for vain sought after dreams!
The Pressures
They thought would be relieved.
The Pressures Of Life
And the way in which
They are perceived;
Determines whether or not
Relief we will have received!
Pressures Of life
Always comes to give us strength,

Giving wisdom to the wise,
That this race of Life
We go the length
Victoriously,
We'll Arise!
TAD 7-20-03 Sun. 3:36 am

Lady In Blonde

Lady in Blonde, Lady In Blonde
Your beauty seems to take me far and beyond.
Your eyes are that of the finest of sapphires;
Your milky smooth skin melts my heart starting an
everlasting fire.
Lady in Blonde, Lady in Blonde
Your magnetism cast a spell
As if you had a magic wand.
Your body is very desirable
And wonderfully made;
More precious than each
And every gemstone
Even the Jade.
Your skin is fairer than the finest of pearls,
Beauty have known you
From the time you were
A virgin girl.
Lady In Blonde, Lady In Blonde
Riches and the extravagance have known you since birth they've
always been aware of your true worth.
Lady In Blonde, Lady In Blonde
Whiter than snow you seem to be, your beauty,
Your beauty is all I can see.
The strength in your legs
Are that of steel,
All I want to do
Is live for your will.

Windy Nights

Windy Nights
Comes in many different ways,
Sometimes the wind blows
For many, many Days.
The wind itself cannot be seen,
It comes sometimes
For your soul to redeem.
What is this that the eyes cannot review?
Without it in the world what would we do?
Windy Nights
The power that it displays
Is known throughout the land.
It moves so swiftly,
It can't be caught
With your hand!
Windy Nights
Causes the mind to drift away;
To a place of no Return
And where it is always day.
Blowing Winds
That passes through the night;
It has no boundaries
Or battles to fight.
Windy days, Windy Nights
They always come
Whether wrong or right.
They can blow so hard they clash and fight;
A cool, cool breeze
Is what they bring;
While sitting in a park, or swinging on a swing.
Like dust in the wind, is how we feel;
Led to the slaughter to the kill.
Blowing too and fro throughout our lives;
Pushed through this world is how it drives.
TAD 6-9-03

Blue Skies

Blue Skies, Blue Skies
You remind me of a window to heaven;
If I had wings to fly
Just imagine what I would Do.
Blue Skies, Blue Skies
Never a hint of dark clouds,
or gloom, the happiness that you display
Is that of a newlywed bride and groom.
Blue Skies, Blue Skies
Without you in my life what would I do?
Bright, sunny and cheerful, also clear as glass;
Blue bright and sunny skies I hope will forever last.
Blue Skies
That are friendly and never gray,
Throughout the night I long to see another day
Hoping and praying the sun will always rise,
Blue Skies and sunny days no one can despise.
Sky Blue Days
Captures my heart
in an endless amount of ways.
Reflecting my life as a mirror
In the sunshine showing its rays.
Blue Skies, Blue Skies
You're bold as the night,
You never come in disguise
Bringing wisdom
To the wise;
Which is never any surprise!
Blue Skies, Blue Skies
Stay around forever and ever,
May the dark gloomy clouds——
come again never never!

Love

Love
What is this emotion?
For which some
Would kill?
Love
Divine sent from God above
It is His only will.
Love
Can often be mistaken;
For lesser emotions it is taken.
Love
Itself is often confused
With the world and Satan's tools.
True Love
For sure comes from up above,
For we all know
God sent His son
Who was wrapped
Within His spirit of Love.
Love Comes from within
The mind, body, spirit and soul,
Nevertheless, but all for the more.
Love
Itself will keep mankind in existence.
Love
Should be sought after
With great, great Persistence!
Love
It magnifies the earth
As if through a looking glass;
Without any love in your life,
Quickly you will fade away.
Love
The earth,
The stars, the planet,
The universe
And more so than ever,
Especially the Heavens

Were created by these emotions;
In the moment
In the twinkling of an eye,
At the gestures of God
And his notion.
Out of Love
He even created Hell.
For those he knew;
Their souls to Satan
They would sell!
TAD 7-20-03 Sun. 5:50 am

AWARDS/ACHIEVEMENTS

 Ted Dyer is an honorary member of the International Society Of Poets. He has just recently been awarded with the 2003 Outstanding Achievement in Poetry Silver Cup award and a Commemorative Medallion Award.

Ted is in the process of writing his second book of poems. Entitled I'm Still Here! He has written several children's books, Johnny The Giant, Andy The Ant Eater, and Little Ricky's First Hair Cut.

0-595-29266-6